The Christian
Interpretation of
the Cabala
in the Renaissance

THE CHRISTIAN
INTERPRETATION OF
the Cabala
IN THE RENAISSANCE

By JOSEPH LEON BLAU

KENNIKAT PRESS, INC./PORT WASHINGTON, N. Y.

To

THE MEMORY OF THE PAST
Rachel Woolf Blau (1875–1932)
Rabbi Joel Blau (1878–1927)

THE JOY OF THE PRESENT
Eleanor Weslock Blau

THE HOPE OF THE FUTURE
Rachael Maya Blau
BORN DECEMBER 14, 1941

FOREWORD

THIS STUDY of types of Christian interpretation of the cabala represents the first attempt at an adequate, balanced treatment of Christian cabalism. There have been fragmentary studies by various authors on which some reliance may be placed. Most writers on the Christian cabala have, however, approached the material from positions of bias and have, therefore, introduced various distortions into their treatment.

Only within the last few years has a study such as this been possible. The work of Professor Gershom G. Scholem of the Hebrew University of Jerusalem, culminating in the recent publication of his masterly *Major Trends in Jewish Mysticism* (Jerusalem, 1941), has cleared the ground for clarified understanding of cabala. I do not hesitate to acknowledge my dependence on Scholem's work for the overall pattern of my thinking about cabala as well as for the many specific points where his work is cited as documentation.

It is the general theme of this book that the use of cabala by Christian thinkers was a fad of no lasting significance; that, no matter what type of interpretation was momentarily aided by cabalistic speculation, this type of speculation rapidly proved a blind alley. That this proved to be so is unquestionably due to the fact that during the very period in which Pico della Mirandola and John Reuchlin and their followers were attempting to utilize cabalistic thought as a basis for their deductive systems, Copernicus, Kepler, and Bruno were building the foundations of scientific systems whose value in use has proved to be so much greater than that of the old systems. Like astrology, alchemy, and other pseudo-sciences, cabala fell a legitimate victim to the development of scientific thinking.

It is difficult, almost impossible, to acknowledge all those to whose assistance I am indebted. I have had the benefit of advice and criticism from Professor Richard McKeon, of the University of Chicago and Professors Irwin Edman, Horace Friess, John Herman Randall, Jr., Salo W. Baron, and Lynn Thorndike, all of Columbia University. Dr. Paul Oskar Kristeller, of Columbia University, saved me from many an error which his fine knowledge of the Renaissance discovered in my work. The trustees of Columbia University by their grant of a University Fellowship in Philosophy for the academic year 1933–34 made possible one year of uninterrupted devotion to this study. The librarians of the New York Public Library, Columbia University Library, the library of the Union Theological Seminary, and the library of the Jewish Theological Seminary have extended to me many courtesies and concessions in the use of their facilities. To all these, I am grateful.

There are three persons to whose encouragement and assistance this book especially owes its completion: Mr. Morris Gabriel Cohen has befriended it and me, has applied his deep understanding to the subject, and has helped me to a formulation of my point of view; Professor Herbert W. Schneider, of Columbia University, has been a tower of strength from the beginning of my work; above all, my wife, Eleanor W. Blau, has been both amanuensis and critic, a source of inspiration and of help without whom I should never have finished this work.

To all these this book owes its virtues and its merits. For its faults and demerits I subscribe myself sole author.

JOSEPH LEON BLAU

Far Rockaway, N. Y.
January 3, 1944

CONTENTS

I

"IN THE BEGINNING"

RELIGIOUS belief may be taken seriously or casually. If it is taken casually, it provides a ready solution to any questions which may arise in the life of the individual. If it is taken seriously, it creates problems—not the problems of the skeptical, leading to the formulation of a rational philosophy, but those of the faithful. True religion, as Bennett pointed out, begins in a doubt. But "the doubt which religion generates is a doubt about the moral relation of the human soul to God. The alternative with which it torments man is not that of God or no God but that of God remote or God near at hand." [1]

This is a problem of religious sophisticates; to the religiously naïve, God's presence is a fact, not a problem—it is a dogma, not a doubt. Religious seriousness commences with a problem created out of the distrust of dogma. The solution of the problem may lead to the reaffirmation of the traditional or orthodox creed; it may lead to that form of religious individualism which we call mysticism; [2] it may lead to the development of an idiosyncratic intellectual construct which satisfies the believer better than simple faith. Those who accept this construct feel themselves set apart from their fellows; they consider themselves to have penetrated more deeply into hidden mysteries; they believe they are the elect. It is to this type of formulation that the term "occultism" is applied.[3]

An occult formulation can develop in any religion; it can best be described as a distortion by exaggerated emphasis of the tradition within which it arose. Thus, though occultism is not orthodox, it is seldom heretical; it vociferates rather than challenges the basic principles of the religion which gave it birth.

[1] Bennett, *A Philosophical Study of Mysticism*, pp. 22–23.
[2] James, *Varieties of the Religious Experience*, p. 379.
[3] Scott, *An Outline of Modern Occultism*, pp. 4–6.

Within the Jewish tradition three major doctrines have received occult emphasis: the doctrine of the transcendence of God, that of the literal inspiration of the Scriptures, and that of the redemption of mankind through the Messiah, son of David.[4] All these doctrines are characteristic of the Jewish culture, although at various times in Jewish history modifications may have entered from the other cultures with which the Jews were in contact.[5]

In the folkloristic narratives of Genesis the presence of God is taken for granted.[6] This anthropomorphic deity represents a thoroughly naïve conception by thoroughly simple folk. If He walks in the garden in the cool of the day, it is not to be marveled at; those who created these legends made God in their own image. Within the same Biblical book, however, we find the patriarchal legends, in which God has become more remote than He was in the earlier tales.[7] He has become deanthropomorphized in these later tales. He must put on human appearance to walk among men, as He did when He visited the tent of Abraham.[8]

The concept of God became more and more refined, more and more remote, less and less human.[9] The prophetic theology, as stabilized into dogmatic formulation by the Pharisees, presented a God supremely eminent. The Palestinian mind was not, however, metaphysical.[10] No matter how exalted God became, He was never conceived as transcendent. His superiority to men in no way affected His direct participation in the government of the world. God's relation to the Jewish people has always been near, and the Jews have looked forward to the day in which that close relationship would be extended to all the peoples of the earth.[11]

The very simplest devices were used in the Bible to rationalize the discrepancy between the eminent God and His immanent activi-

[4] Scholem, *Major Trends in Jewish Mysticism*, p. 11. My review of this book in *Review of Religion*, VIII (1943), 67–77, details the points on which I differ from Scholem.

[5] See Franck, *Kabbalah*, pp. 213–307, for some suggestive material on these influences.

[6] Gunkel, *Legends of Genesis*, pp. 8–9.   [7] *Ibid.*, p. 13.   [8] Genesis xviii.

[9] The peak of this movement, it seems to me, is to be found in Deutero-Isaiah. Noteworthy, in particular, is the theology of Isaiah xl. 12–26.

[10] Moore, *Judaism*, I, 360.   [11] *Ibid.*, p. 423.

ties. Whether the rationalization took the form of calling Abraham the Friend of God, or of describing Moses as seeing God face to face while the people waited at the foot of the mountain, or of asserting that the Jews were a chosen people, the explanations are of an extremely uncritical nature—not those of the religiously sophisticated. Even in the relatively sophisticated setting of the book of Job, the Lord, speaking from close at hand, out of the whirlwind, defends Himself against a charge of mismanagement by asserting His eminence.[12]

Not until the Jew was placed in a philosophically keener environment, in Alexandria, did the concept of transcendence, toward which the Jewish view of the nature of God had been unconsciously moving, enter openly into the theological picture. Not until then was the reconciliation of the two aspects of God by reason rather than by faith necessary. The problem of serious religion, of which Bennett spoke in the passage quoted earlier, became acute. The solution proposed by Philo of Alexandria was elaborated along the general lines of middle-Platonic thought. It took the form of a theory of emanation.[13]

In later Jewish thinkers, such as the Karaite, Benjamin of Nahawend (fl. 800–820),[14] the aspect of transcendence was stressed almost to the exclusion of the aspect of immanence. This led to an increasing need for the adaptation of the Philonian system by providing that both the creation and the government of the world be carried on by means of intermediaries who are themselves creations, rather than emanations, but whose power emanates from God.

In the form of the doctrine of the *sephiroth*, emanation theory became central to cabalistic thought. The *sephiroth* combine both

[12] Job xxxviii–xli.
[13] See Goodenough, *By Light, Light*. This work should be used with great caution.
[14] See the excellent summary of the work of this Karaite leader by Samuel Poznanski in the third volume of the Hebrew encyclopedia *Otzer yisrael*, New York, 1909. The treatment in Graetz, *History of the Jews*, III, 153–54, is not particularly valuable. The work of Benjamin exists only in fragmentary form; most of our information about him comes from the historical work of Kirkisani. His system involved the direct creation by God of the higher angels only; these, in turn, created the lower angels, who created man. Strictly speaking, it is a doctrine of intermediacy rather than a theory of emanation. In his own time the relation between Benjamin and Philo was recognized, although Graetz allows no Jewish source for his work.

aspects of previous emanation theories; they reveal God to the earnest seeker through gradually more exalted attributes and thus provide a way from man to God; they are also the intermediaries by means of which God's intervention in human affairs takes place, and thus they provide a way for God to man.[15]

The doctrine of the literal inspiration of the Scriptures is the second basic element in our definition of cabalism. The post-exilic Jew made of the Scriptures a rallying point for his downcast national pride.[16] Every form of his religious life had to be based upon the absolute sanctity of the Torah; the Torah as a whole and in every part was divinely inspired or divinely revealed.[17] Literal adherence to this divine document provides a thoroughly satisfactory solution to the problem of authority for the naïve religionist.

To the more sophisticated, however, this doctrine poses a problem instead of bringing a solution. The Scriptures contain much material which can by no stretch of the imagination be considered sacred. Furthermore, many of the legal sections of the Torah had reference to the specific conditions of a particular time and were either inapplicable or unnecessary at a later period. Finally, the impact of changed conditions on the life of the Jews, both in Palestine and in Diaspora, demanded new laws for situations for which the Torah made no provision. The problem of religious sophisticates was how to make the Scriptures at one and the same time more sacred and more effective. The search for a solution led to the development of an exegetical system of a highly complicated type, involving the assumption that there is a deeper sense lying hidden beneath the letter of the Scriptures.[18] Literal adherence to the Scriptures could be maintained only by disregarding literal interpretation.

In its orthodox setting, among the Tannaim, the Amoraim, and their later descendants the Rabbinites, this exegetical technique has meant the production of a vast literature of commentary on the Bible, culminating in the Talmud, on which, in turn, the lavish exercise of ingenuity has produced commentary and supercom-

---

[15] Scholem, *Major Trends in Jewish Mysticism*, p. 13.
[16] Herford, *The Pharisees*, p. 58.   [17] Moore, *Judaism*, I, 247–48.
[18] *Ibid.*, p. 248.

mentary, all by a sort of dialectic legerdemain. The doctrine of literal adherence has been more honored in the breach than in the observance; to describe the Jews as "the people of the Book" is to use poetic rather than precise terminology.

The Karaite movement may have represented a shift from this spurious and casuistic literalism back to a genuine regard for the letter of the law.[19] It has been maintained, too, that the cabala arose primarily in opposition to Rabbinic casuistry and is marked by a return to the simple doctrine of literal inspiration.[20] If this was true, it did not remain so. Not only did cabalists accept all the hermeneutic rules of the Talmudists; they also added other exegetic techniques, of which the technique of interpretation by means of the symbolism of numbers loomed so large that at least one author considered this the whole of cabala.[21] Any technique of exposition or exegesis which will establish every word of the Bible on an exalted plane is acceptable to the cabalist. Such exaltation is a necessity, for there is much in the Bible which is too trivial to be the work of the Supreme Intelligence. It is necessary to determine the hidden meanings lying behind superficial trivialities. Furthermore, it is evident that, like the Rabbinites, the cabalists, by insisting on the doctrine of literal inspiration, developed an exaggerated respect for the letter as such, that is, for the exact form in which the Scriptures were handed down. In some forms this respect was amplified into an occult theory of creation in which the letters play an active part.[22]

It is, perhaps, fairest to say that the cabalists, like all other mystics and occultists in the Jewish tradition, maintained stanchly the traditional belief in the Divine Revelation. They asserted, however, that this revelation was a dual one. They averred that Moses received both the text of the Scriptures and a technique for interpreting the text at the same time. So exhaustive was this technique that by its aid not merely was every word of the Scriptures fruitful,

[19] This is the thesis of Cahn, *Rise of the Karaite Sect.*
[20] Karppe, *Etude sur les origines et la nature de Zohar,* p. 228.
[21] Barth, writing of the cabala of H. C. Agrippa; see chap. vi, *infra.*
[22] The basic document of this approach is *Sefer Yetzirah* (*The Book of Formation*), which begins: "In thirty-two mysterious paths of wisdom did the Lord write . . . *He created His Universe by the three forms of expression: Numbers, Letters, and Words.*" Stenring's translation; my italics.

but every syllable, every letter, every punctuation mark, every ac-
cent, every elongation or prolongation introduced by the scribes for
the creation of a beautiful manuscript was also credited with both
sanctity and meaning and served to reveal some hidden aspect of the
infinite power of God.[23]

Of the cabalistic doctrine of redemption there is far less to say,
because in its original form, in the earlier cabalistic works, it is simply a reiteration of the traditional Jewish doctrine of the Messianic
Age.[24] Briefly stated, the Jewish doctrine of salvation excluded the
idea of personal redemption. When the world is ready, there will
come an age of truth, justice, and mercy for all the righteous, led
by the Messiah-who-shall-come, the descendant of David. It is
definitely a this-worldly doctrine; it predicates, not a heavenly paradise, but an earthly paradise. Only in the later forms of cabalism
did an untraditional element, metempsychosis, enter deeply into
the cabalistic scheme, not as a substitute for, but as coexistent with
the traditional doctrine.[25]

In the combination, then, of three doctrines and the speculative
outgrowths of these doctrines, a medieval Jewish occultism was
born. This occultism is called "cabala," which means "tradition."
It need surprise no one that an exact date cannot be set for its incep-
tion. None of the ideas incorporated into the cabala was completely
unexplored in earlier Jewish mysticism. The early cabalists simply
brought together a great many ideas which had been developing
for more than a thousand years.[26]

Now, even if we admit the medieval origin of cabala as a system,
we must admit that it had many predecessors and precursors, both
in Jewish and in non-Jewish thought.[27] Among the non-Jewish
sources, Scholem refers particularly to the Gnostic sects; [28] Adolph

[23] Scholem, *Major Trends in Jewish Mysticism*, p. 14.
[24] See Moore, *Judaism*, II, 279–395, for a very full presentation of this doctrine.
[25] This doctrine is, it is true, present in a remote form in the very early *Bahir*, but
is made little of in cabalistic texts down to the time of Luria. It is only in his works
that transmigration becomes fundamental in cabalistic thought.
[26] Adler, "Kabbalah," in *Jahrbücher für spekulative Philosophie*, II (1847), 393.
[27] Philipp Bloch, *Entwickelung*, p. 1.
[28] Scholem, "Zur Frage der Entstehung der Kabbala," in *Korrespondenzblatt*, IX
(1928), 4–26; see also Scholem, *Major Trends in Jewish Mysticism*, chap. ii.

Franck leans to the "theology of the ancient Persians," although he recognizes that this hypothesis required the ascription of great age to the cabala; [29] Bension presents a rather superficial account of the influence of Moslem and Christian mysticism on the development of the Zohar.[30]

Baron, however, tends to minimize these analogies as accidental products of the similar operation of the minds of mystics and to incline to a belief in a Jewish origin of cabala.[31] Graetz makes a similar point, but less sympathetically, asserting that cabala arose in the opposition to the rationalist philosophy of Maimonides.[32] Adolph Jellinek points to two possible earlier Jewish sects as sources of cabalistic ideas: the sect of "Jehudim," who maintained that the inner and the outer senses of the Scriptures were distinct, in opposition to whom Sa'adia (d. 942) wrote, and the sect called "Makariba," which was concerned largely with angelology and made much of the angel Metatron.[33] If this sect is identical with the sect al-Magghariya, called by Graetz "the Makaryites or Maghariyites," this is another line bringing cabala back into the orbit of Benjamin of Nahawend, for al-Magghariya was a group of followers of his doctrine.[34]

Concerning the age and the early development of the cabala then, there is no agreement among those who have made it their special province. When, however, cabala emerges openly upon the stage of history, it is possible to be somewhat more specific about its development. Broadly, in the pre-Zoharic period (before 1300), three schools of cabalistic thought can be distinguished.[35]

The first of these, the school of Isaac the Blind (fl. 1190–1210) and his disciples Ezra and Azariel, developed the doctrine of emanations and suggested the doctrine of metempsychosis. This group functioned chiefly in the south of France and in Spain. The school of Eleazar of Worms (fl. c.1220) introduced the elements of number

[29] Franck, *Kabbalah*, pp. 306–7. [30] Bension, *The Zohar;* especially, pp. 28–75.
[31] Baron, *A Social and Religious History of the Jews,* II, 135–48.
[32] Graetz, *History of the Jews,* III, 565–76.
[33] Jellinek, *Beiträge zur Geschichte der Kabbala,* I, 53–56.
[34] Graetz, *History of the Jews,* III, 153–54.
[35] See Karppe, *Zohar,* pp. 237–306; Graetz, *History of the Jews,* III, 565–76; Baron, *History of the Jews,* II, 135–48.

and letter symbolism and the practical cabala which later loomed so large in cabalistic thought. The school of Abraham ben Samuel Abulafia (1240–c.1292) combined and developed the materials of its predecessors in both practical and theoretical cabala. To this school belonged Joseph ben Abraham Gikatilia (c.1247–1305), whose works formed the major background of John Reuchlin's studies in the cabala. Gikatilia's work was far more systematic than any which had been done before his time and was noteworthy for the attention he paid to the development of the techniques of gematria, notarikon, and themurah.

Gematria was a very ancient device.[36] It involved the use of the fact that in ancient languages, including Hebrew, the letters of the alphabet also represented numbers. This suggested that, when the sum of the numerical equivalents of the letters of two or more words was the same, the words might be considered identical and used interchangeably.[37] Without restriction as to language, since both Latin and Greek were susceptible of this treatment, as well as Hebrew, the Christian cabalists could produce virtually any interpretation they desired. The work of Reuchlin shows this use at its peak by a writer entitled to be taken seriously.

Notarikon,[38] an acrostic system, was employed in various ways. The initial or final letters of the words of a phrase might be joined to form a word which was then given occult significance. The significance of another word might be explained by expanding it into a phrase, using each letter of the original word as initial letter of one word of the phrase. Finally, two words might be joined as one and thus given new meaning; strictly speaking, the latter method should not be considered as notarikon.

Themurah, which means "transposition," is actually a combina-

---

[36] Hopper, *Medieval Number Symbolism*, pp. 62–68, presents evidences for the antiquity of gematria, dating the name at about A.D. 200, but claiming a far earlier beginning for the system.

[37] Trachtenberg, *Jewish Magic and Superstition*, pp. 262–63, discusses this technique, with some examples. That gematria also provided a source of entertainment and was, in fact, a favorite "parlor game" among the medieval Jews is asserted by Abrahams, *Jewish Life in the Middle Ages*, pp. 381–82.

[38] Trachtenberg, *Jewish Magic and Superstition*, p. 314*n*, allows the derivation of this word from the Latin *notarius*, a writer of shorthand.

tion of the letter substitutions of the code and the anagrammatic inter-change of the resultant letters. Since an alphabet of twenty-two consonants provides twenty-one codes, and since vowel sounds are not printed in Hebrew, an almost infinite number of letter combinations can be produced from any one Hebrew word, and some few of these combinations are likely to form words. This method, then, is likely to be fruitful.

Gikatilia also systematized the doctrine of the *sephiroth*, or emanations, which the followers of Isaac the Blind had developed.[39] It is in the form of his systematic presentation that the *sephiroth* entered Christian thought.

As it was stated in the Hebrew sources, the doctrine of the *sephiroth* was that the Supreme and One God, the boundless, the limitless, the *En Soph*, by a voluntary retraction or self-limitation, manifested Himself in the highest of the *sephiroth*, *keter*, the crown. This was not God; it was, however, a manifestation through which God could be seen "as in a glass, darkly."

From *keter* there were three emanations, producing three more *sephiroth*, each of which represented a manifestation of God at a level of grossness further removed from His sublimity and transcendent Being. Further regression produced the complete system of ten emanations, of which the last was *malchuth*, the kingdom.[40] The entire group of ten emanations was repeated on four different levels, or realms, so that there were forty regressions from God to our world. These were the worlds, or realms of emanation, creation, formation, and material action. A variant scheme, which seems to be more closely related to non-Jewish thought, limits the number of worlds to three, the worlds of angels, celestial bodies, and elements. This is the presentation of this subject given by Menahem Recanati. When the Scriptures referred to God as remote, it was as the unknowable source of the entire series; when God was appar-

[39] Azariel ben Menahem (c.1160–1238) was a pupil of Isaac the Blind and the author of *A Commentary on the Ten Sephiroth by Means of Questions and Answers*, which is summarized in Jellinek, *Beiträge*. Another treatise of this school, *A Treatise on the Emanations*, supposedly written by R. Isaac Nasir in the first half of the twelfth century was published in Jellinek, *Auswahl kabbalistischer Mystik*, Part I.

[40] Gikatilia, *Sha'are orah* (*Gates of Light*), develops this scheme.

ently treated as present, it was actually one of the lower manifestations which was known to man.[41]

At this point in the development of the cabala, at about the end of the thirteenth century, there was first presented to the world that document which is preëminently considered central to the cabala, the Zohar, the "book of splendor." The Zohar is not a single book; it does not develop a consistent system, but behind its repetitious and discursive comment there lies a theosophical doctrine which is a riot of lush esotericism.[42] The Bible commentary of Menahem ben Benjamin of Recanati (c.1290–c.1350), which was the major source of Pico della Mirandola's cabalistic knowledge, is actually a commentary on the Zohar. Recanati was the foremost of the group of cabalists who have been called "the school of the Zohar" and combine and absorb all the features and doctrines of all previous schools in a planless, unsystematic fashion.

The high point of this cabalistic movement came between the twelfth and the sixteenth centuries, and its most distinguished writers all came from the countries bordering on the Mediterranean. It was here that cabala assumed its most philosophic form.[43] Its finest expression came in the work of Moses Cordovero (1522–1570) who wrote in Safed, in Palestine. His *Garden of Pomegranates* systematized and integrated all the speculative elements of cabalism to his time.[44]

As far as it is possible to do so briefly and in the light of the fact that the study of the cabala is in a "prescientific stage," [45] the his-

[41] Scholem, "An Inquiry into the Kabbala of R. Isaac ben Jacob Ha-Cohen," in *Tarbiz*, III (1931), 33–66, is the fullest source of information on this matter. On p. 59 Scholem ascribes the first statement of the doctrine of four worlds to R. Isaac ben Samuel of Akko (fl. 1290) in the unpublished *Meirath 'enayim*, which is among the Hebrew works on cabala included by Elia del Medigo (1463–1498), one of the Hebrew teachers of Pico della Mirandola, in an autograph list published by Dukas, *Recherches*, pp. 55–66. For Recanati, see Scholem, "An Inquiry," in *Tarbiz*, III (1931), 58–59.

[42] The authorship is not definitely known. It is the consensus of modern opinion that it is a pseudepigraph of the thirteenth century, ascribed by its actual author, Moses ben Shem Tob de Leon (d. 1305), to R. Simon ben Yochai, a Palestinian Tanna of the second century A.D. For a full and excellent account see Scholem, *Major Trends in Jewish Mysticism*, chaps. v–vi.

[43] Karppe, *Zohar*, p. 236.   [44] See Appendix A, below.

[45] Baron, *History of the Jews*, III, 125n.

tory of the cabala is here sketched during the period when it has a bearing on the subject of this study. Some of its major doctrines have been presented in the context of history, and some indication has been given of the most important sources used by Christian writers.

At this point an attempt should be made to list the most important doctrines of the cabalists in such a way that later references to these doctrines will not be read in isolation. Such a listing, for the reasons which appear from the historical survey, is a matter of extreme difficulty.

First, a distinction should be made which appears among the Hebrew cabalists and gained great favor with their Christian followers. This was the distinction between *ma'aseh bereshith*, the work of creation, and *ma'aseh merkavah*, the work of the chariot. These terms appeared in Jewish thought far earlier than did the movement with which they have become associated.[46] *Ma'aseh bereshith* includes all the cosmological speculations and creation myths of the cabalistic tradition; among the others, the *sephirotic* doctrine looms large. It is necessarily based primarily on the first chapter of Genesis. With the slight reinterpretations which were sketched earlier, it fits into a Christian pattern.

Ma'aseh merkavah, however, based on the interpretations of the vision of the chariot in Ezekiel, introduced the eschatological speculations of the Jews. These, despite the attitude of the more rationalistic Jews,[47] essentially supported the Messianic formulation of the official Jewish religion. The Messiah-who-shall-come and the hour of his coming and the nature of his rule on earth were their subjects.[48]

The cabalists maintained that God is boundless in His nature and cannot be grasped by human reason because He is without will, intention, desire, thought, language, and action. He is an Infinite Being, utterly and completely unknowable and inconceivable in His

[46] See Moore, *Judaism*, I, 383–84, for a discussion of *ma'aseh bereshith*, and pp. 411–13 for *ma'aseh merkavah*; Sjöberg, *Gott und die Sünder*, pp. 244–48, adds some interpretative comment of value; Scholem, *Major Trends in Jewish Mysticism*, chap. ii, contains an excellent treatment of *merkavah* mysticism.

[47] See Maimonides, *Mishneh Torah* I. ii. 12, *et passim*, where the term is used as a synonym for metaphysics.

[48] Silver, *A History of Messianic Speculation*, discusses these matters in detail.

infinity, containing all perfection and all existence in Himself. He
is an absolute and utterly incomprehensible unity. He is called *En
Soph*, the Infinite.[49]

God cannot be the direct creator of the world, for a creation proceeding directly from Him would have to be boundless and perfect,
He, therefore, begot ten emanations, or *sephiroth*, which form the
Adam kadmon, or archetypal man. The *sephiroth* form the highest
of four worlds, the world of emanation, *aziluth*. From this world
evolve successively the world of creation, *beriah*, the world of formation, *yetzirah*, and the world of making, *asiyah*. Each of these is sub-
divided into ten ranks, paralleling the ten *sephiroth* in the highest
world.

All human souls are preëxistent and occupy a rank in the world of
aziluth. God made room for other beings by a voluntary contraction
and shrinking of Himself. This is known as *zimzum*. These souls of
men temporarily inhabit the *kelifoth*, or husks known as the human
body, which is also made after the archetypal pattern.

No one has seen the *En Soph* at any time. The anthropomor-
phisms of the Scriptures refer to the *sephiroth*. Men can never come
into direct contact with the Deity until all the preëxistent souls shall
have passed through the appropriate probationary period. If any
soul, in its passage through life on this earth, fails to develop the
seeds of perfection which are planted in it, it must return to earth
in a different body. However, to aid in the return of all souls to their
Infinite Source, a strong soul may voluntarily join a weaker soul in
one body, and the two souls proceed through life together. This is
the doctrine of *gilgul*, metempsychosis.

The various divine names are not arbitrary combinations of
sounds; they conceal a mystery of miraculous power in their letters.
So, too, do the names of the angels. By uniting these names and com-
bining their letters in various ways, men may achieve the power to
influence the course of nature and to bring about miracles. All these
doctrines are concealed in the Holy Scriptures. Knowledge of the
proper techniques of interpretation is the key to release a secret
meaning from beneath the literal surface.

[49] Ginsburg, *The Kabbalah*, p. 145; P. Bloch, *Geschichte der Entwickelung die Kabbala*, p. 3.

During the years between 1480 and 1650 many Christian think-ers and writers made use of cabalistic materials in one fashion or another. It is the intent of this study to distinguish several of the major types of use to which these materials were put in the works of some of the more important Christian interpreters of the cabala. In gauging the importance of the writers chosen for treatment the author has been guided partly by chronological criteria and partly by the frequency with which these writers were quoted as authorities in the works of later scholars, as well as by the interest of the use each made of cabalistic materials.

The study of the Bible and the study of classical humanities were the poles between which the Christian interpretation of the cabala arose. For the study of the Bible led to the study of the Hebrew lan-guage, an indispensable prerequisite to the study of the cabala. The study of the classical humanities brought up the task of reconciling ancient thought with the Christian tradition. By an easy extension, which was largely also necessary because so many of the classical texts were transmitted through Arabic sources, the study of Arabic and Hebrew texts came to be included in the program of the human-ists, and therefore the study of the Semitic languages came into prominence.[50]

These languages had to be studied if much cabalistic material was to be read, for very little was available in Latin translation during the period under consideration. We are told in various places of translations of cabalistic manuscripts at the request of Pope Sixtus IV.[51] We learn, too, of three Latin translations in the hand of Egidio di Viterbo, written in 1513, and therefore possibly translated con-siderably earlier.[52] Paul Ricci was the author of a translation of Gikatilia's *Sha'are orah* (*Gates of Light*), completed about 1510 and known at least to Reuchlin. *Sefer Yetzirah* (*The Book of Forma-

[50] Anagnine, *Pico della Mirandola*, p. 107, discusses this question in relation to Pico. Reuchlin and Ricci taught both Hebrew and Greek. On the Christian Hebraists see the fine bibliographical note in Baron, *History of the Jews*, III, 136–38, and the supplementary materials listed in Baron, *Bibliography of Jewish Social Studies*, pp. 109 ff., 235 f.

[51] For example, in Pico, "Apologia" (*Opera*, I, 123), and in Gaffarel, *Codicum cabbalisticorum manuscriptorum*.

[52] Dukas, *Recherches*, p. 60.

tion) was made available in two translations during the sixteenth and seventeenth centuries, one the work of Guillaume Postel,[53] the other of John Stephen Rittangel.[54] Postel also made a translation of some sections of the Zohar, but this was never printed. Thus, it is evident that if much was to be read of cabala, the languages of the original texts, Hebrew and Aramaic, had to be mastered.

Once it was recognized by the men of the Renaissance that there was such a doctrine as the cabala, it had to be investigated and as far as possible integrated into the syntheses they were formulating. For with the expansion of man's terrestrial horizon which served as prelude to our own era, new tendencies in thought became evident. The glory of Renaissance humanism was its breadth, not its depth. The questing minds of the period could not rest until they had looked under every tombstone in the cemetery of old systems of thought and had brought to light any concealed treasure which might be added to their synthetic world picture.

For the Renaissance, like our own age, was eclectic; the humanists of the Renaissance refused to limit themselves to any one system of thought, no matter how sanctioned or by whom. Rather did they insist, as Francis Bacon did in England, that all knowledge was their province. As men of action in the Renaissance explored the earth to discover new countries, as men of science explored the skies to discover a new universe, men of thought explored the world of ideas to discover new systems. And as the explorers made the new countries into temporal empires, making the ends of the earth their own, the humanists made the new systems into intellectual empires, making all thought their own. In this ferment the Christian interpretation of cabala was one current among many seething currents and crosscurrents.

The Hebrew cabala made an excellent subject for the type of treatment given by these seekers of synthesis. It was early recognized among the Jews that some of its positions were dangerously close to Christian belief, and much of the opposition to it stemmed from this correspondence. When Pico della Mirandola was led to the study of the cabala by his Hebrew teachers and friends, he found

[53] Paris, 1552.   [54] Amsterdam, 1642.

its adaptation easy. All that had to be done was to substitute the Christian doctrine of the Messiah-who-had-come for the Jewish doctrine of the Messiah-who-shall-come, to substitute Jesus, a concrete redeemer who had already been on earth, for the vague future redeemer believed in by the Jews. It was not difficult to adapt the doctrine of literal inspiration of the Scriptures, since the cabalistic techniques for deriving the hidden meanings in the text were equally apt for the discovery of Christian implications. When the Christian interpreters took over *ma'aseh merkavah*, they had to wrench it out of its Jewish framework and to make of it a theosophical structure supporting the doctrine of the Messiah-who-had-come. This was done by substituting the Book of Revelation for the apocalyptic books of the Jews, thus formulating a Christian "work of the chariot." This is probably the most drastic change which these interpreters had to make.

The doctrine of creation by remote control, as represented in the *sephiroth*, presented, superficially at least, more of a problem, because this scheme does not seem to allow of easy interpretation into Christian doctrine. From the time of Pico, however, it was adapted into the Christian system by considering the three highest *sephiroth*, *keter*, *chochmah*, and *binah*, as the representations of the Trinity. *Keter*, the supreme diadem, represented the Father; *chochmah*, wisdom, represented the Logos, the Son; *binah*, understanding, heading the left-hand column of mercy, became the representative of the Holy Spirit of Grace. The only other emanation which was treated with any thoroughness was the sixth of the *sephiroth*, *tifereth*, glory, which was conceived as the representation of Jesus incarnate. Thus, if anything, the doctrine of the *sephiroth* aided the Christian interpreters of the cabala, for it gave them the opportunity to distinguish between the Son as the divine wisdom and the Son as the incarnate redeemer; it also resolved the difficulty of explaining the triune God by making the persons of the Trinity manifestations or emanations of the Limitless God, by considering the Father, the Son, and the Holy Spirit as Three out of One, rather than Three in One.

Among the aspects of cabalistic speculation which were more interesting to the Christian interpreters who followed Pico were the three main techniques of Scriptural interpretation. These, rather than the manipulation of the *sephiroth*, established the application of cabala to Christianity. These three methods were known to the Hebrew cabalists as gematria, notarikon, and themurah. Perhaps in the long view it is more important that by their identification of Jesus with the sixth of the *sephiroth*, and the Son of God with the second, and God Himself as the *En Soph*, while attempting to justify Trinitarian dogma, they actually weakened Trinitarianism.

The authors who are presented here started an intellectual fad. In their own lifetimes they saw their ideas spread far and wide across Europe. The spreading, the diffusion, took place partly because of their books, partly by direct contact, and partly because of the activities of their opponents. However spread, the ideas were widely synthesized with and often indistinguishably introduced into various Platonic systems of thought.[55] The fad flamed, flickered, and finally faded. After a brief period cabala no longer seemed to provide serious religionists with an answer to their problems. After this period the entry of new elements converted Christian cabalism into something other than it is here, into a vague groping toward theosophy.

[55] Nicolson, "Milton and the *Conjectura cabbalistica*," *The Philological Quarterly*, VI (1927), 1–2.

II

THE PHOENIX OF HIS AGE

THE BEGINNINGS of cabalistic study among the Christian humanists are somewhat more definite than its beginnings among the Jews. The Christian interpretation of the cabala started during the last quarter of the fifteenth century. It is not possible to say who was the first scholar to mention cabala. Some knowledge of it seemed to develop almost simultaneously in several places.

One error of the past can, however, now be relegated to the limbo of forgotten faiths. Raymond Lull (1232–1316) did not write of cabala in the thirteenth century.[1] Thorndike's suggestion that the manuscript of the pseudo-Lullian treatise *De auditu kabbalistico* is written in a fifteenth-century hand brings us to the period of this study.

De auditu kabbalistico is not evidence of a great knowledge of cabalistic materials; it shows a realization that the name "cabala" means tradition;[2] it asserts that since every doctrine and discipline must be considered under three heads, namely, its parts, its desired end, and the means to that end, so cabala must be presented in this systematic fashion. The divisions which are given do not, however, represent the cabala.[3]

The first section of the book deals with the alphabet, and because it presents a form of letter mysticism it approaches the alphabetic techniques of cabala. The nine letters B, C, D, E, F, G, H, I, and K are associated with the nine qualities, good, great, lasting, powerful, wise, ready, virtuous, true, and glorious, which were declared to be the "parts of the subject."[4] The text goes on to speak of the "figure" called A, which is circular or spherical, that called T, which represents three triangles, the third figure, composed of A and T, to sig-

---

[1] See Appendix B, below.
[3] *Ibid.*, pp. 3–4.

[2] *De auditu kabbalistico*, p. 1.
[4] *Ibid.*, pp. 5–6.

nify that whatever is implied in them is implied in it; and the fourth figure, composed of three circles of which the largest is fixed, the other two mobile.[5]

This is as close as the author of *De auditu kabbalistico* comes to the cabala, save in the name of the tract, and this is by no means cabala. It is, in a sense, fortunate that the experience of meeting the word "cabala" used with little similarity to its true meaning comes so early, for it warns against the easy assumption that the writers who will be discussed in this study were all experts in the field.

At all events, this is indication of an early familiarity with the name "cabala," though an exact date is lacking. Another such vague, early reference is supplied by Thorndike, who refers to Martin Polich of Mellerstadt (d. 1513), who "engaged in disputations concerning the Cabala," but gives no date for these disputations or any reference which might help to clear up the nature of Polich's material.[6] Jacques le Fevre d'Etaples (c.1455–1536) refers to cabala in his *Natural Magic*.[7]

Still another group of references is to be found in Lodovico Lazarelli's *Crater hermetis*, and this can at least be dated by a *terminus ad quem*. It must have been written before 1494, when Ferdinand of Naples, to whom the work was dedicated, died.[8] Lazarelli (1450–1500) was not completely without a background of Hebrew literature; although his frequent allusions to Philo, who "was a Hebrew and very wise," do not reveal a knowledge of Hebrew,[9] his references to Moses Maimonides,[10] to a treatise "Abuda Zara" [11] and to "bresith Raba" [12] indicate either that the author was himself widely read or that he had available sources of information about the texts he cites.

Since Lazarelli lived for some time in Rome, he had available a source of information in the Jews of that city. That he took advantage of some such opportunity is indicated by his references to the

---

[5] *Ibid.*, pp. 6–18.
[6] Thorndike, *History of Magic and Experimental Science*, IV, 455. See also Bauch, *Geschichte der Leipziger Frühhumanisten*, pp. 8–9.
[7] Lefevre d'Etaples, *De magia naturali* II. 29.
[8] See Kristeller, "Marsilio Ficino e Lodovico Lazzarelli."
[9] Lazarelli, *Crater Hermetis*, ff. 63v; 68r; 70r.
[10] *Ibid.*, f. 68r.   [11] *Ibid.*, f. 73r.   [12] *Ibid.*, f. 71v.

Zohar [13] and to *Sefer Yetzirah*.[14] Again, in this exposition by question and answer, when the king asks what is the soul of man, Lazarelli replies, "on the authority of the mecubales or cabalists of the hebrews," that the light of God is the soul of man, a phrase which may have been used by cabalists, but was actually from the book of Proverbs.[15] Finally, there is indication that the author has some notion of the relation of magic to cabala, an understanding of cabala as oral tradition, and a knowledge of others beside himself who were conscious of the existence of cabala.[16]

Then, too, the existence of manuscript translations of cabalistic materials into Latin by Jews is evidence that in the last quarter of the fifteenth century an interest in cabala was developing. The Assemani catalogue describes several cabalistic manuscripts translated by the Jew Flavius Mithridates.[17] Kristeller has found a manuscript translation of Joseph Gikatilia's *Sha'are zedek* (*The Gates of Justice*) which belonged to Pico.[18] Pico himself refers to a translation of cabalistic manuscripts, undertaken for Pope Sixtus IV.[19] This may or may not be the same as those listed by Assemani.

All the evidence thus far has been concerned with the establishment of the period in which a Christian interpretation of the cabala can be said to have arisen. Some of the work mentioned may have preceded Pico della Mirandola's studies in the cabala; some may have followed. There can be no question, however, that it is with the work of Pico that this section should be concerned.

In the first place, whatever had been done before his time, it was Pico who first attracted his fellow humanists in any considerable number to the cabala. His contemporaries and immediate followers with one accord agree with his statement that he was the first of the Latins to have mentioned cabala.[20] It is particularly noteworthy that Pico's interpretation of the cabala gained so firm a hold on the minds of his period that Ricci, writing about 1510, had to defend his far

---

[13] *Ibid.*, f. 68v.   [14] *Ibid.*, f. 78v.

[15] *Ibid.*, f. 72r. See Proverbs xx. 27.   [16] *Crater Hermetis*, ff. 79v–80r.

[17] Assemani, *Bibliothecae Apostolicae . . . catalogus*, pp. 155–61.

[18] See Kristeller's review of Anagnine in *Civiltá moderna*, X (1938), 4.

[19] Pico, *Opera*, I, 123.

[20] *Ibid.*, I, 180. See also Reuchlin, *De arte cabalistica*; Galatinus, *De arcanis*; and other works cited in later chapters.

more competent work in the cabala against the accusation that it was
not cabalistic, because he had included material which Pico did not
mention.[21]

In the second place, the type of use made of the cabala by Pico is
most interesting. For him it was one element, perhaps the most important, in a universal synthetic system of thought. It is, therefore,
with the content and the influence of Pico's cabalistic knowledge that
this section is concerned.[22]

When Pico was very young, perhaps because Pico was very young,
he decided to bend his efforts to the reconciliation of all known systems of thought. In preparation for this adventure he drew up a
series of nine hundred theses, derived from various sources, and announced his willingness to defend any or all of these against any
scholar who cared to enter the intellectual lists.[23] Included among
the nine hundred were forty-seven theses drawn from Hebrew cabalistic sources [24] and seventy-two other propositions involving
Pico's own deductions from these sources.[25]

With the introduction to this section of original theses, we come
to an important aspect of the study of cabala by Christians; that
aspect, in fact, which justifies the use of the phrase "Christian interpretation of the cabala." For Pico announces his own deductions as
"seventy-one [sic] cabalistic conclusions according to his own opinion, derived from the fundamental ideas of the Hebrew sages,
greatly strengthening the Christian religion." [26] The primary intention of the Christian interpretation of cabala, as first shown in the
earliest of the Christian interpreters, was to seek for new means of
confirming the truths of the Christian religion; and Pico makes the
point, in one of the first of these propositions according to his own

---

[21] See, on this point, chap. v, note 18.

[22] Much has been written about Pico's Hebrew teachers, Elia del Medigo, Jochanan
Alemanno, and Flavius Mithridates. A recapitulation of the conclusions and controversies of the writers would serve little purpose here. The best of the material is
to be found in Cassuto, *Gli Ebrei a Firenze*, pp. 316–26, and Anagnine, *Pico della
Mirandola*, pp. 74–104. Other literature is cited by these writers.

[23] J. F. Pico, *Ioannis Pici . . . vita*, in Pico, *Opera*, I.

[24] Pico, *Opera*, I, 80–83.   [25] *Ibid.*, I, 107–13.

[26] *Ibid.*, I, 107. See also Garin, *Pico della Mirandola*, p. 152.

opinions, that a Hebrew cabalist must inevitably agree with the doctrine of the Christians in the matter of the Trinity.[27]

The men of the Renaissance did not lose faith in their religion when they rediscovered the past. For many, the primary task was to produce a justification of their faith which would include both the old justification and the new material. Much of the apparent instability of the philosophy of the period must be charged to the sincere efforts of philosophers to supply this revised rationale for Christianity while still assimilating newly rediscovered classical philosophies. Within this atmosphere, under the spur of Pico's enthusiasm, a group of his successors attempted to base Christianity on cabala. Scholem has said that Jewish mysticism is concerned with the interpretation of the idea of God, as He is manifested in creation, revelation, and redemption. The Christian interpretation of cabala attempts to fuse a specifically Christian concept of the Divine act of redemption through Jesus with the concepts of creation and revelation common to both Judaism and Christianity.

Pico's forty-seven derivative theorems are, as might be expected, concerned with creation and revelation. Though he does not here enter into a discussion of the precise schematization of the *sephiroth*, or the "paths of wisdom," or the "gates of intelligence," he shows that he knew the schema and that he knew of its relation to creation.[28] His statement of the principle according to which the cabalist viewed revelation, that is, the revealed Scriptures, is sufficiently interesting to merit quotation: "There are no letters in the entire Law which do not show forth the secrets of the ten *sephiroth* in their forms, conjunctions and separations, curvature and directness, deficiency and superfluity, smallness, and largeness, their crowning, their closed or open form, and their arrangement." [29] Every letter in the Scriptures contains a revelation beyond its literal significance. This superrevelation has nothing to do with the meaning of the passage under consideration. It depends on such factors as the size, shape, and decoration of the letters of the sacred text in the sacred

[27] Pico, *Opera*, I, 108.
[28] *Ibid.*, I, 80–83, Nos. 3–6, 8, 10–11, 13, 17–18, 25–26, 28, 36.
[29] *Ibid.*, I, 82.

language. To the cabalists Hebrew was unquestionably the sacred language, "language in its purest form" which "reflects the fundamental spiritual nature of the world." [30] There is no doubt that Pico agreed, for he calls Hebrew "the first, and original language." [31]

When we consider Pico's seventy-two original propositions, we leave creation and revelation behind and enter into the realms of redemption.[32] It becomes the purpose of our author to prove the Messiahship of Jesus and to a lesser extent the sanctity of the Trinity, by the adaptation of cabalistic ideas. Here, too, we meet two significant phrases, repeated at every questionable point: "Whatever other cabalists say, I . . ." and "No Hebrew cabalist can deny . . ." [33] Thus we learn that "no Hebrew cabalist can deny" that the cabalistic interpretation of the name Jesus is "God, the Son of God, and the wisdom of the Father through the third person of divinity" [34] and again that the Tetragrammaton refers to "God, the Son of God, made man by the Holy Spirit." [35] Pico's use of such phrases makes it evident that he anticipated disagreement, because he realized that he was going not merely beyond his sources, but even into a different universe of discourse. He was creating a Christian interpretation of the cabala.

Evidences of Pico's dominant interest, the reconciliation of all philosophies, are not lacking in the nine hundred theses. He realized, for example, that the apparent differences were in many cases merely terminological; many of his conclusions are therefore equations of names in one system to names in another, perhaps better-known system. Thus, the *sephiroth* are identified with the planetary system in one theorem,[36] and in a later theorem are equated with a psychological scheme.[37] The variety of such possibilities makes it

[30] Scholem, *Major Trends in Jewish Mysticism*, p. 17.
[31] Pico, *Opera*, I, 89, No. 80. I have discussed an interesting later manifestation of this belief in "Foreshadowings of Phonetics," in *The Spoken Word*, III (1935), 12–13.
[32] Pico, *Opera*, I, 107–13, Nos. 5–8, 14–15, 19–27, 30, 32–34, 37–43, 45–47, 51–52, 54, 61–62.
[33] "Quicquid dicant alii (caeteri) Cabalistae, ego" and "Nullus Hebraeus Cabalista potest negare."
[34] Pico, *Opera*, I, 108, No. 7.   [35] *Ibid.*, I, 109, No. 15.
[36] *Ibid.*, I, 111, No. 48.   [37] *Ibid.*, I, 113, No. 66.

easy to understand the appeal that the cabalistic system of *sephiroth* held for Pico.

Another aspect of this tendency is the direct equation of single terms from one system to another. "Typhon" in the "Orphic" system is the same as *Zamael* in cabala; [38] "night" in the Orphic system is equated with *En Soph* in cabala; [39] the "other life" of the *Epinomis* is the "neutral world" of the cabalists; [40] what Themistius calls "the active illuminating intellect" is just the same as Metatron in cabala.[41]

Another type of relationship is indicated by Pico's comments on the statements of the Chaldean interpreters of the aphorisms of Zoroaster:

The words of the Chaldean interpreters on the eleventh aphorism concerning the double drunkenness of Bacchus and Silenus are perfectly understandable in the light of the words of the cabalists concerning the twin wine.[42]

What the interpreters say about the fourteenth aphorism can be perfectly understood by what the cabalists say about the death of the kiss.[43]

He who reads in the book *Bahir* what is the affinity of she-goats and lambs with the spirits knows what is to be understood by she-goats in Zoroaster.[44]

In these theses the dogmas of one system are used to indicate the clarification of those of another system.

Finally, there is the attempt, to which reference has already been made, to defend the Christian faith in terms of extraneous systems of thought.

Whatever miracle occurs, whether it be magical, or cabalistic, or of any other kind whatever, it is principally to be referred to God, the glorious and blessed, whose grace daily pours down freely supercelestial waters of miraculous powers upon contemplative men of good will.[45]

[38] *Ibid.*, I, 107, No. 13.   [39] *Ibid.*, I, 107, No. 15.   [40] *Ibid.*, I, 97, No. 32.
[41] *Ibid.*, I, 73; "Secundum Themistium," No. 2.
[42] *Ibid.*, I, 104, No. 6.   [43] *Ibid.*, I, 104, No. 7.
[44] *Ibid.*, I, 104, No. 15. Kibre, *The Library of Pico della Mirandola*, found that Pico's collection included a copy of *Sefer ha-bahir*.
[45] Pico, *Opera*, I, 104–5, No. 6.

The works of Christ could not have been accomplished by either magic or cabala.[46]

There is no science which makes us more certain of the divinity of Christ than magic and cabala.[47]

Thus we see how Pico tried to make the God in whom he believed at once superior to and dependent upon other systems than the one of which this God is the apex.

Pico's nine hundred conclusions were produced in 1486, were read and talked about, but they never came to public debate as their author had hoped they would. The ecclesiastical authorities stepped in to prevent that. They accused Pico of heresy in thirteen of the conclusions. An examining commission was appointed to consider whether the heretical views were actually present in the suspected conclusions. The commission was chosen with extreme care to include a representative of each possible point of view within the church.[48]

Hastily Pico prepared to defend himself against the specific charges. He composed his *Apologia*, dedicated to Lorenzo de Medici. He wrote with less care and perhaps less tact than was necessary, showing some of the impatience of youth with its slower-moving elders. Somewhat flippantly, he charged his accusers with unthinkingly standing firm for the retention of their own viewpoint and with being unwilling to have materials which they would have to study, ideas with which they were unfamiliar, approved as authoritative.[49]

Disregarding Pico's defense against those accusations which have no bearing on our subject, we proceed to his defense on the question of natural magic and cabala. "The fourth conclusion condemned by them was this: 'There is no science which makes us more certain of the divinity of Christ than magic and cabala.' "[50] First, Pico points

---

[46] *Ibid.*, I, 105, No. 7.   [47] *Ibid.*, I, 105, No. 9.

[48] Dorez and Thuasne, *Pic de la Mirandole en France*, pp. 61–63, contains a full list of the members of the commission and their ranks and dignities.

[49] For the *Apologia*, see Pico, *Opera*, I, 114–240. Most of the flippancy can be found in the introductory remarks, pp. 114–25.

[50] Pico, *Opera*, I, 166.

out that in using the word *scientia* he is, of course, referring to non-revealed knowledge. His conclusion was in no sense a derogation of theology, which is revealed truth and therefore not under consideration.[51] In accordance with this phase of his argument, he rewords the conclusion thus: "Magic and cabala make us more certain of the deity of Christ than other nonrevealed sciences." [52] Later, he makes the far more cautious and safer statement: "There is no science, extending the name of science to both revealed and nonrevealed knowledge, which makes us certain of the divinity of Christ, except the evangelical doctrine and the science of Christian theology." [53]

After defending his belief in "natural" magic, which he carefully distinguishes from necromancy, Pico enters upon a fuller, but no more systematic, statement of his cabalistic knowledge, chiefly with reference to the interpretation of numbers.[54] Here he refers to the Introduction to the *Apologia*, where he has told of the seventy cabalistic books which the previous pope, Sixtus IV, had had translated into three Latin volumes. At this point Pico tells which Christian doctrines he thought proved by cabala, out of these translated works. His list includes the mystery of the Trinity, the Word made flesh, the divinity of the Messiah, original sin and its expiation through Christ, the heavenly Jerusalem, the fall of the demons, the orders of the angels, expiations, and punishments in hell.[55]

Pico's *Apologia* was not satisfactory to his judges, and since Jean Cordier, later rector of the University of Paris, cast the sole dissenting vote, they declared him guilty of heresy. He was cleared only after a special appeal had gained the pardon of the pope.[56] One of the judges, Pedro Garzia, bishop of Ussel, feared that he might be accused of disregarding evidence; to safeguard himself, he published at Rome, in 1489, a résumé of the evidence and of his conclusions therefrom and addressed this little work to the pope.[57] Controversy breeds controversy. Pico found a stalwart champion in Archangelus of Borgo Nuovo, a Franciscan monk,[58] who wrote one

---

[51] *Ibid.*, I, 168.   [52] *Ibid.*, I, 167.   [53] *Ibid.*, I, 239.
[54] *Ibid.*, I, 173–81.   [55] *Ibid.*, I, 123.
[56] Dorez and Thuasne, *Pic de la Mirandole en France*, p. 63.
[57] *Ibid.*, pp. 188–95.   [58] See Appendix C.

volume in defense of Pico's derivative cabalistic conclusions,[59] and a second volume in defense of Pico's cabalistic propositions "secundum propriam opinionem." [60] A third book by this writer is an expansion of Reuchlin's concluding chapters to *De verbo mirifico*.[61]

The second work, in its published form, is preceded by the *Apology* of Archangelus for undertaking a defense of cabalistic doctrine. Here the author asserts that two laws, one written, the other oral, were revealed to Moses. Thence the written law was given to the people; the oral law was handed down from generation to generation, transmitted through the seventy elders, the Prophets, and the Men of the Great Synagogue, until it reached the hands of Rabbi Jehudah ha-Nasi, who wrote down part of the tradition in the six books of the *Mishnah*.

Meanwhile, however, the tradition had been known before Moses, and parts had been written in several books; one of them, *Sefer Yetzirah*, written by Abraham, has come down to us. These books contained the mysteries of the cabala. At this point in his discussion Archangelus quotes Reuchlin to the effect that the survival of one work proves that the others existed.[62]

There follows a list of "cabalistic" doctors: some of them are not cabalists; [63] some are given credit for writings of which their authorship is at least dubious; [64] and some are in general rationalistic in their methods of procedure, though they may have written occasional mystical passages or made use of such techniques as gematria.[65] There are also cabalists listed. The list seems to have been taken in part from Georgius [66] and in part from Reuchlin.[67] This derivation from Reuchlin is particularly evident; Archangelus perpetuates one of Reuchlin's favorite errors by listing R. Joseph ben Abraham Gikatilia under two separate names, as two separate writers: R. Joseph Carnitole and R. Joseph Cicatilia.

[59] Archangelus, *Cabalistarum selectiora, obscurioraque dogmata.*
[60] Archangelus, *Apologia . . . et conclusiones cabalisticae numero lxxi.*
[61] Archangelus, *Specchio di salute.*   [62] Archangelus, *Apologia*, p. 10.
[63] For example, Bachya ibn Pakoda, author of *The Duties of the Heart.*
[64] For example, the ascription of the Zohar to R. Simon ben Yochai.
[65] For example, R. Joseph Albo, author of *Ikkarim.*
[66] See the discussion of Georgius, *De harmonia mundi*, below.
[67] See chap. iv.

At the conclusion of the list there is an exaltation of this very same writer under yet another name, "Rabbi Joseph Bar Abraham Castiliensis civis Salernitanus," who wrote with clarity, in his book entitled *Genat agoz*, about the interpretation of words, letters, and punctuation.[68]

Archangelus then proceeds to make a distinction between "opus de beresith," or natural philosophy, and "opus de mercava," or spiritual science.[69] While the distinction between *ma'aseh bereshith* and *ma'aseh merkavah*, creation and the "chariot" is stressed by almost all who write on the cabala, the interpretation of creation as natural philosophy and of the "chariot" as spiritual science is an unusual twist, which is derived from Pico's division of cabala into alphabetic permutation and the triple *merkavah*.[70] This is only understandable if we realize that by "natural philosophy" both Pico and Archangelus meant a metaphysics of nature, an occult science "explaining the powers of created things, both natural and celestial." [71] Furthermore, we must understand that by "spiritual science," or the triple *merkavah*, Pico meant knowledge of the divine names and the *sephiroth*, of angelic powers, and of stones and herbs, that is, of alchemy.[72]

Archangelus next introduces, following Reuchlin, a discussion of the two worlds on which cabalists and Talmudists agree, *olam haba* (the world to come) and *olam haze* (this world). His interpretation makes of *olam haba* the intellectual world to which the cabalist seeks to rise and of *olam haze* the sensible world, that lower level on which the Talmudist remains.[73] The cabalist is not, like the Talmudist, bound to the letter of the Scriptures; he seeks to rise to the intellectual world by learning the true meaning of the words of God.[74]

To conclude his own *Apologia*, Archangelus parallels Pico's *Apologia*, with a statement of the Christian doctrines which he believed proved by cabala. These include the doctrines of the Trinity, of the

---

[68] Archangelus, *Apologia*, p. 11.   [69] *Ibid.*, p. 12.

[70] Pico, *Opera*, I, 108, No. 2.   [71] Archangelus, *Apologia*, p. 12.

[72] Anagnine, *Pico della Mirandola*, pp. 110–14, is a full and illuminating discussion on this point.

[73] Archangelus, *Apologia*, pp. 13–14.   [74] *Ibid.*, p. 15.

dual nature of Jesus, of original sin, of redemption through the
passion and blood of the Messiah, of the resurrection of Jesus, of
the beneficent virgin, queen of heaven, of the mystical body of
the Church, of the Last Judgment and the destruction of the world,
of penitence and the remission of sins, of the resurrection of the
dead, of the prophetic gift of knowledge and wisdom, of allegorical
interpretation, and of the spiritual sense of the Scriptures.[75] This is
a fuller list than that produced by Pico and, as might be expected
from a professionally religious scholar, somewhat more complete
in technical details.

The commentaries of Archangelus on Pico's conclusions are full
and not of great importance. They serve to emphasize the point
made by Gaffarel [76] in the seventeenth century and by Anagnine [77]
in the twentieth that the major source in Hebrew cabalistic literature for the conclusions of Pico was the Bible commentary by Menahem Recanati. It is important to mention this only because Menahem's commentary is not an original work but a simplification of
the Zohar. Pico's source may be said, therefore, to be a watered-down
version of the cardinal document of the cabala. The Zohar, however,
is thoroughly unsystematic; it is a lush and luxuriant jungle of
mystical ideas, often brilliant, often mutually inconsistent. The same
comment would apply, to a lesser degree, to Pico's conclusions.[78]
Cabala may be the key to Pico's system, as Dreydorff suggests,[79] but
where is the key to his version of the cabala?

Another work by Pico, which was extremely important in his time,
is his *Heptaplus*,[80] a rather rhapsodic treatment of the Biblical account of creation.[81] Although this work is broadly symbolic, it is
cabalistic only with respect to the doctrine of the worlds therein

[75] *Ibid.*, p. 14.   [76] Gaffarel, *Codicum cabalisticorum manuscriptorum, passim.*
[77] Anagnine, *Pico della Mirandola, passim.*
[78] On the question of system or lack of it in the conclusions of Pico see the brilliant
analysis by Cassirer, "Pico della Mirandola," in *Journal of the History of Ideas*,
III (1942), 123–44; 319–46. Cassirer also points out the symbolic nature of Pico's
thought, which explains in large measure why he was attracted by cabalistic
speculation.
[79] Dreydorff, *Das System des Johannes Pico*, p. 17.
[80] "Heptaplus," in Pico, *Opera*, I, 1–62.
[81] Pico's work was, for example, used by Colet in the preparation of his *Letters to
Radulphus on the Mosaic Account of the Creation*. See Seebohm, *Oxford Reformers*,
p. 34, and Lupton, ed., *The Letters to Radulphus*.

presented.[82] This is the doctrine of three worlds of intelligences, of celestials, and of elementaries, which was earlier associated with the name of Recanati.[83] To these three Pico adds a fourth world, man himself.[84] It is significant that Pico does not mention the cabalists in all the *Heptaplus*, though he does cite the Talmudists. The conclusion must be that the work is not cabalistic. In fact, Pico himself suggests that even his statement of the doctrine of worlds was derived, not from the cabalists, but from classical antiquity.[85]

Considering the place of the cabala in Pico's thought, it is remarkable how slight a mark his cabalistic studies left on his correspondence. There are only four letters preserved which contain any direct reference to his Semitic studies.[86] Of these four, only a letter to an unknown friend refers directly to the cabala. The letters to Corneus and Ficinus speak in general terms of the study of Hebrew and related languages. In a letter to an unknown friend Pico mentions the antiquity of *Sefer Yetzirah*, to which he refers as *Abraham de creatione*, and says that the cabalistic authors clarify the divine mysteries. This is, however, incidental to the chief purpose of the letter, which is to answer some specific questions about the Chaldaic alphabet and about the dubious passage in Josephus which mentions Christ. Apparently the conclusion to be drawn from this lack of cabalistic reference in Pico's letters is that he was striking out into unknown fields where his correspondents were left behind.

When we come to the letter of May 30, 1492, to Pico's nephew, there is food for much speculation. Even here the facts are meager. On or about May 23, 1492, Pico gained possession of some Hebrew books, which he then studied day and night.

---

[82] Cassuto, *Gli Ebrei a Firenze*, p. 323, insists that the work is cabalistic, while Garin, *Pico della Mirandola*, p. 151, as stoutly denies this.

[83] Pico, *Opera*, I, 7. See chap. i for the association of this doctrine with Recanati; chaps. v, vii, and viii for its expression by Agrippa, Thenaud, and others.

[84] Pico, *Opera*, I, 8. This idea was also borrowed by Thenaud; see chap. vii.

[85] Pico, *Opera*, I, 5–6, referring specifically to Plato's "Phaedrus."

[86] Pico, *Opera*, I, 376–79, Letter to Andreas Corneus, October 15, 1486; pp. 376–78, Letter to Marsilio Ficino, from Fratta, 1486; pp. 384–86, Letter to an Unknown Friend, from Fratta, November 10, 1486; p. 360, Letter to his Nephew, May 30, 1492. There is also a letter, published among others by Pico, from a Vatican manuscript, by Dorez in *Giornale storico della letteratura italiana*, XXV (1895), 352 ff., which deals in vague terms with the charges against Pico's thirteen allegedly heretical propositions.

This is the reason I have not hitherto answered your letters: certain Hebrew books fell into my hands, with which I have been busy for an entire week, every day and every night, till they have almost blinded me. A certain Sicilian Jew who brought the books here is going to leave in about twenty days, so don't expect to hear from me until I have extricated myself from them. I can't possibly spare a moment from them, lest by chance they leave before I have examined them all. When I'm free from this care, I'll overwhelm you with letters; you know I have a very busy mind.[87]

Superficially, this is not so very important. Pico is so busy with a group of Hebrew books lent him by a Sicilian Jew that he has no time to write to his favorite nephew. But when the date of this letter, May 30, 1492, is considered in the light of that other date, March 31, 1492, on which the decree expelling the Jews from Spain and her territories, including Sicily, was promulgated by Ferdinand and Isabella, the letter takes on new meaning.[88]

For the wholehearted devotion with which Pico was absorbed in these books suggests that they were completely new to him, despite his friendship with many Italian Jews. The Jews who were driven from Spanish territories were permitted to take all their movable property except money and articles made from silver and gold.[89] We know, too, that many of the Sicilian Jews came to Italy.[90] What is more probable than that through the good offices of his Italian Jewish friends Pico was enabled to borrow these books from a transient Sicilian Jewish refugee?

What Pico learned about cabala from these new sources, unfortunately, he did not record. Had he lived to remold his thought along lines suggested by them, it is conceivable that the entire direction of the Christian interpretation of cabala might have been changed. The remaining two years of his life passed, however, with no written contribution to cabalistic thought; it is to the works of others that we must now turn to find traces of Pico as mediator and introducer of cabalism to the Christian world.

[87] Pico, *Opera*, I, 360.   [88] Graetz, *History of the Jews*, IV, 372–74.
[89] Marcu, *The Expulsion of the Jews from Spain*, p. 148.
[90] Joshua Bloch, *Hebrew Printing in Naples*, p. 4, and the literature cited by Bloch.

III

OUT OF THE ASHES
OF THE PHOENIX

WE HAVE SEEN that, whereas Pico deserves the credit for being the first successfully to present the study of cabala to the Christian world and his studies in cabala were extensive for a pioneer, his actual writings on the subject were limited, unsystematic, and obscure. Perhaps this was due to his early death, perhaps to the taint of dilettantism which weakened so much of the scholarship of his time.

His influence on his contemporaries and on those who came after him, however, goes far beyond the limits of his own writing. The most important of his converts was, of course, his older contemporary John Reuchlin, whose cabalistic works will be analyzed in detail later in this study.[1] The commentaries of the Franciscan Archangelus of Borgo Nuovo have already been mentioned. Beyond these men Pico's direct influence spread as far as England, and it persisted until the middle of the seventeenth century.[2]

Among the earliest of those who followed Pico down the tortuous ways of cabalistic thought was the Franciscan Franciscus Georgius, of Venice, whose religio-philosophical poem, published in 1525, took for its subject nothing less than the harmony of the whole world.[3] Following a suggestion by Pico,[4] Georgius refers to the parallel between the cabalists and the Pythagoreans.[5] This suggestion is one that impressed Reuchlin, who thought that his studies in the cabala were the means for resurrecting the study of Pythagorean-

---

[1] See below, chap. iv.
[2] Some details of the later spread of Pico's influence can be found in Blau, "The Diffusion of the Christian Interpretation of the Cabala in English Literature," in *The Review of Religion*, VI (1942), 146–68.
[3] *De harmonia mundi totius cantica tria.*
[4] Pico, *Heptaplus*, in *Opera*, I, 1–2.   [5] *De harmonia mundi*, p. iir.

ism.[6] For Georgius, however, this was not enough. The harmony which he sought was of the nature of Pico's synthesis of all philosophies. Georgius, therefore, soon followed the suggestion that cabala and Pythagoreanism are parallel by the suggestion, which, it is just to remark, is left in tentative form, that there is a correspondence between the ten *sephiroth* and the ten Aristotelian categories.[7]

Georgius explains that there have been many writers in the cabalistic tradition, and he presents a long list,[8] similar in many respects to that given by Reuchlin in *De arte cabalistica* and later repeated by Archangelus in his *Apologia*. It is notable that the similarity goes beyond the names cited; precisely the same descriptive phrases are used.[9]

There is much of importance, says Georgius, to be learned from the letters, points, and accents of Sacred Writ.[10] He applies the numerical mysticism of the gematria to different names of God in various places in his text.[11] He discusses the names of God associated with the *sephiroth* and the numerical equivalence of the *sephiroth*.[12] At the beginning of his second book Georgius adds the interesting point, derived from Pico and paralleled in Archangelus, that "the name of God is the same as God Himself; and the power of the Divine Name is identical with the power of God, if the sages of the Hebrews are correct." [13]

Once more in Georgius, as in Pico and in Archangelus, we find some slight knowledge of cabala, based upon a limited number of sources and used even more than it was in Pico as decoration for a universal, eclectic system. The harmony of the whole world is like a metrical scrapbook, more or less topically arranged. Wherever Georgius found a flower in his reading of Latin, Greek, or Hebrew sources, he plucked it and placed it in his *De harmonia mundi*, with no regard to its consistency with its surroundings.

Somewhat more satisfactory is a tiny prayer and commentary composed by the learned Augustinus Justinianus Genuensis (1470–

---

[6] Reuchlin, *De arte cabalistica* (in Pistorius, *Artis cabalisticae*), p. 612.

[7] *De harmonia mundi*, p. viir.   [8] *Ibid.*, pp. xxxv–xxxir.

[9] See Archangelus, *Apologia*, p. 11.   [10] *De harmonia mundi*, p. lxxvr.

[11] For example, *ibid.*, pp. lxxxixr–v; ccliiv–ccliiir; *et passim.*

[12] *Ibid.*, pp. xcviir–xcviiiv.   [13] *Ibid.*, p. cxcir.

1536), bishop of Nebia, and published first in 1513 under the title *A Prayer Full of Piety to the Omnipotent God Composed of the 72 Hebrew and Latin Divine Names; together with an interpretative commentary.*[14]

The first part is a hymn and prayers developing seventy-two attributes from the seventy-two names of God; all comment and interpretation comes in the second part. Here we learn that Justinianus, though geographically and politically closer to Pico, had gone either to Reuchlin or to a Hebrew source behind Reuchlin or, possibly, to Gikatilia's *Sha'are orah,* in the Latin translation by Paul Ricci, for the point is made that the seventy-two names are based upon the conjunction of verses 19, 20, and 21 in Exodus xiv.[15]

Other indications of Justinianus's familiarity with Hebrew cabalistic sources can be found in his *Polyglot Psalter.* Here, in a gloss on Psalm ciii, *Sefer Yetzirah* on the *sephiroth* is quoted; reference is made to a cabalistic manuscript in the glosses on Psalms cxxxvi and cxxxix. *Siphra ditzenioutha,* one of the minor tractates of the Zohar, is quoted in glosses on Psalms i, vi, xlix, and cvi. References to other Hebrew sources are also numerous and indicate that Justinianus was a far more competent Hebraist than most of his contemporaries in that his acquaintance with Hebrew literature went beyond the Scriptures.

Despite his use of cabalistic material and his knowledge of its source and of the nature of cabalism, Justinianus was not certain whether to consider Judaism religion or superstition.[16] He recognized that followers of cabalistic doctrine have led virtuous lives,[17] but dissociated himself completely from the wonder-working, magical, theurgical uses of the names of God.[18] Good bishop that he was, he would not compromise his orthodoxy for a mess of miracles.

A long jump carries our inquiry into England, at the beginning

---

[14] Justinianus, *Precatio pietatis plena.* The entire text is reprinted as a gloss on Psalm cxix, in Justinianus's famous *Psalterium,* an early polyglot edition, containing the earliest life of Columbus, inspired by local patriotism, as a gloss on Psalms xix. 4. This life should be consulted by more of those who rush to print with intuitive statements about the biography of Columbus.

[15] Justinianus, *Precatio,* p. Bir. See Ginsburg, *Kabbalah,* pp. 132–36, for a full explanation of the permutations of these verses to derive seventy-two names.

[16] *Precatio,* p. Biiir.   [17] *Ibid.,* pp. Biiv–iiir.   [18] *Ibid.,* p. Bvir.

of the sixteenth century, where the ferment of the Italian Renaissance had long been working in a group including John Colet
(1466–1519). To this English group, humanistic in character, the
Renaissance meant chiefly the revival of the study of Greek. Colet
studied in Greek the works of the pseudo-Dionysius. In the year
1497, shortly after his return from a two-year visit to Italy, Colet
composed *Two Treatises on the Hierarchies of Dionysius*,[19] in
which he had occasion to discuss the cabala.[20] His discussion goes
farther than mere dependence upon Pico; it is practically a word-
for-word transcript of a passage from Pico's *Apologia*.[21] Immediately after this passage drawn from Pico, Colet goes on, still without mentioning Pico's name, to say: "Pope Sixtus IV with great zeal
provided a translation of them [cabalistic books] into Latin by the
aid of some learned man [Pico]; and in his lifetime three volumes
were under perusal." [22]

Though Colet walked at first in the cabalistic footsteps of Pico,
he did not limit himself to the reading (and rewriting) of Pico's
works. From a letter which he wrote to Erasmus in 1517 we learn
that Colet also read Reuchlin's *De arte cabalistica*. Erasmus, who,
as we see from his letter to Albert, archbishop of Brandenburg
(November 1, 1519), had scant respect for the cabala,[23] sent a
copy of Reuchlin's book to John Fisher, bishop of Rochester. This
annoyed Colet, who wrote to Erasmus:

[19] These treatises remained in manuscript until 1869, when they were published
with an introduction, notes, and translation by J. H. Lupton.

[20] Colet, *Hierarchies*, pp. 236–38, for the original; pp. 109–11 for the translation.

[21] That the correspondences are too close to be accidental is evident from the passages appended. The italics are mine. Pico: Mosem non *legem* modo, *quam quinque
exaratam libris posteris reliquit*, sed *secretiorem* quoque et *veram legis enarrationem
in monte divinitus accepisse* . . . *at mysteria secretiora, et sub cortice legis rudique
verborum praetextu latitantia, altissimae divinitatis arcana, plebi* palam facere,
quid erat aliud, quam dare sanctum canibus, et inter porcos spargere margaritas.
Colet: Moyses quidem non tantum *legem, quam exaratam quinque libris posteritati
reliquit*, sed etiam certe *in monte* Syna *divinitus accepit* totius *legis secretam et
veram enarrationem*, interpretationemque, et sensum spiritalem apertae. *At* vero
secretiora illa *mysteria, et sub cortice legis rudique praetextu verborum latitancia,
archana* videlicet illa *altissimae divinitatis* si veteres illi stultae *plebi* patefecissent; id,
te quaeso, *quid fuisset aliud quam sanctum dare canibus et inter porcos spargere
margaritas.*

[22] Colet, *Hierarchies*, p. 111.   [23] Erasmus, *Opera*, III, 514 A–B.

I'm somewhat angry with you for another reason, too; you sent Reuchlin's book on cabala to Rochester, and not to me. Not that I wouldn't want it sent to him; but that I wish you had sent one to me at the same time. For I take such pleasure in your love that I suffer when I see you less mindful of me than of others. That book came into my hands first, and it was read by me before it was given to Rochester. I dare not evaluate the book. I know my own ignorance and how blind I am about matters so remote and the works of such a man. As I read, however, much of it seemed to me to be greater miracles of words than of deeds; for (as it shows) I know not what mysteries Hebrew words have in their characters and combinations. Erasmus, my friend, of books and of knowledge there is no end.[24]

Colet, however, is doubtful of the value of cabala, particularly in its relation to its use as a sure way to salvation. His doubt leads him to reiterate the traditional means of assuring salvation, and he concludes the letter with the statement: "In my opinion, we shall attain this in no other way than by ardent love and imitation of Jesus. By this means, having left the by-paths, let's get to truth by a short-cut." [25]

John Fisher (1459–1535), who received the book from Erasmus, learned at least the word "cabala" and the idea of an oral revelation paralleling the written "Scriptures." If he read Reuchlin's book at all carefully, he must have learned a great deal more. In Fisher's sermon against Luther, delivered in 1521, he uses and explains the word "cabala" twice.

Saint Paule sayth . . . Almyghty God the fyrst persone in the godhed many dyvers wayes instructed our fathers by his prophetes. Saint Paule meaneth here by our fathers the Iewes. Of whom we spiritually descended. for Abraham that was theyr carnal fader is oures also spiritual. Now Almighty God the father taught them by his prophetes, whose prophecyes all be it they be wrytten in scrypture. yet was there many moo thynges which they spoke unwritten that was of as grete authoryte. as that that was wryten which the mayster of Iewes calleth cabala, which is derived fro man to man. by mouthe onely & not by wrytynge.[26]

Se than I saye what we haue to conferme those thynges that be taught vs by the chyrche. Fyrst the prophetes that were instructed by the father

[24] Allen, *Opvs epistolarvm Des. Erasmi*, II, 599.
[25] *Ibid.*   [26] Fisher, *English Works*, p. 332.

almyghty god. and also theyr Cabala. that is too saye theyr secrete eru-
dycyons not wryten in the bybble . . .[27]

An interesting, if slight, extension of Pico's influence is to be seen
in the work of Peter Bongus (d. 1601).[28] His book, *The Mystical
Meaning of Numbers,* quotes Pico's *Apologia* and *Heptaplus* frequently to establish authority for the mystical meaning of a certain
number. Bongus also explains the number thirty-two, important in
cabalistic speculation because it is the number of the "paths of intelligence," according to the interpretation given in "Lib. de forma-
tione," which is the *Sefer Yetzirah.* So casual, however, is Bongus's
acquaintance with cabala that the ten *sephiroth* do not appear under
the mystical meanings of the number ten.[29] Despite this lack of
information, the author has no scruples about asserting in his Preface
the dependence of Pythagoreanism upon cabala, undoubtedly basing
this contention upon the authority of Pico, Georgius, and Reuchlin
rather than upon the study of original sources. His statement is,
however, unequivocal: "Almost all the philosophy of Pythagoras
was derived from the cabalists." [30]

Not only was a fancied similarity between Pythagorean and cabalistic thought elevated into a direct relationship, but, as we have
seen in Pico, every possible system was searched for parallels with
cabalism. One system very close in nature to cabala was Neoplato-
nism, which may actually have entered into the background out of
which cabala developed. It was this Platonic system to which the
activities of Marsilius Ficinus and the others, including Pico, in the
Florentine Academy acted as spurs. Needless to say, the revival of
Platonism created employment for many heresy hunters. Therefore, especially among the Dominicans, as we have seen, all products
of Platonic thinking were subject to rigid scrutiny. The time was
ripe for a guide to Plato based on orthodox doctrine.

One such guide was supplied by Johannes Baptista Crispus, of
Naples (d. 1595), in the form of a lengthy and extremely erudite

---

[27] *Ibid.,* pp. 335-36.

[28] Bongus, *Mysticae numerorum significationis,* Bergamo, 1585.

[29] *Ibid.,* II, 8.

[30] *Ibid.,* from the unpaged Preface to the Reader. The guiding hand of Pico and
very nearly his exact words are evident in this section.

treatise on the wary reading of Plato.[31] Crispus is extremely wary;
each section of his book starts with a résumé of the heresies and
heterodoxies which are to be discussed therein, and a list of authorities, chiefly patristic, against these heresies. In the course of twenty-
three subdivisions all the major problems of philosophy in his time
are considered.[32]

In discussing the matter of the creation of the rational soul by
God,[33] Crispus addressed a "digression to those who affect the name
of more secret theologians." [34] Among those who like to be called
"more secret" (Crispus would say "more superstitious") theologians [35] are the cabalists. That the ideas of Pico were the source of
much of the information which Crispus gives in this section is indicated by the fact that he discusses forms of different occult systems
in the same pattern as that in which they are presented by Pico. Thus,
the cabalistic *En Soph* and *Zamael* and the Orphic "nox" and
"Typhon" are discussed together by Crispus, just as they were
equated by Pico,[36] and the various names of God which the cabalists
associate with the *sephiroth* are here placed in conjunction with the
names of the planets, as Pico places the *sephiroth* and the planets
together in his conclusions.[37] The entire digression simply repeats
ideas we have met before and is intended to show the dangerous
pitfalls of occult thought concealed in Platonism, avoidable only by
a wariness equal to the author's.

Among the other Renaissance Platonists who dabbled in cabalism
was Cesare d'Evoli, of Naples, who published in 1589 a slight
treatise, *De divinis attributis quae sephirot ab Hebraeis nuncupantur.*

[31] Crispus, *De Platone caute legendo*, Rome, 1594.
[32] I quote the list as it appears: "De Deo, De Uno, De Ente, De Divinis et internis
productionibus, De Aeternitate creaturae, De Mente, De Ideis, De Anima mundi,
De Aeternitate, De Rerum Creatione, De Intellectibus, De Diis Iunioribus, De
Materia, De Daemonibus, De Caelo, De Tempore, De Motu, De Mundo, De Dei
Providentia, De Fato, De Fortuna, De Anima Rationali et Bruta, De Homine, De
Rebus naturalibus, De Rebus politicis, De Malo, De Summo Bono." This list indicates the probability that this work was particularly directed against Patrizzi,
Nova de universis philosophia.
[33] Crispus, *De Platone caute legendo*, Part 1, Book II, pp. 31–56.
[34] *Ibid.*, pp. 44–49.   [35] *Ibid.*, p. 44.
[36] *Ibid.*, p. 49. See also Pico, *Opera*, I, 107.
[37] Crispus, *De Platone caute legendo*, p. 47. See also Pico, *Opera*, I, 111.

This work is notable in that it defends the cabalistic system as an improvement on the Platonic ideas. The defense is maintained by references to Plato and Aristotle. First D'Evoli proves that the attributes must be either God Himself or a projection of God. That they are not God is clear, for God is indivisible by reason, while they are divisible by reason.

Therefore necessarily they are powers or emanations proceeding from God, like rays out of the substance of the sun; wherefore, if rays are instruments . . . the attributes are like some sort of instruments to God . . . The rays of the sun are perceived by sense . . . God, since He is most simple and free from all material and material conditions, cannot have instruments; truly he ought to be known through instruments.[38]

So he shows that the attributes must be instruments of God by means of the Unmoved Mover. They are, he then maintains, an improvement on the Platonic ideas, because each of the attributes has a different character, whereas all the Platonic ideas are of like character.

In closing a section which presents briefly the work of a few writers whose attention was directed to cabalism and whose notions of the cabala were formed by Pico, who appeals to us not so much because of his work as because he died pathetically young, before the promise he showed could reach its true fruition, it is appropriate that another similar to Pico should be displayed. Charles Montecuccolus (fl. 1600) died when he was not quite nineteen years of age we are told by his brother Francis; yet he knew Latin, Greek, Hebrew, and Chaldean and was familiar with all the sciences. He began to produce books in the fields of philosophy, theology, astronomy, mathematics, and cabala in his fourteenth year, and he wrote widely in all these fields until about his eighteenth year.[39]

Our precocious Charles tried to make his slight introduction to cabala systematic. He divided his work into seven chapters:

1. What cabala is; what are its essential doctrines; and whence it came
2. Concerning the divisions of this science
3. That the human body is called microcosm

[38] D'Evoli, *De divinis attributis*, pp. 4–5.
[39] Montecuccolus, *In cabalam introductio quaedam*, "Introduction," p. 12.

4. Concerning the powers of the "Sefirod" and their brilliance, which the holy Fathers and the Prophets got from them

5. Concerning the four worlds

6. The method of prayer which the ancient prophets used to get in contact with the power of the "Sefirod"

7. Treats of the mystery of the Eucharist, which was seen in the spirit and announced by the old-time cabalists.

In his first chapter Charles refers to *Pirke aboth* (*The Ethics of the Fathers*) to show how the tradition was handed down.[40] He accepts the Mosaic origin of the tradition, and for its importance he quotes Pico's conclusion that "There is no science which makes us more certain of the divinity of Christ than magic and cabala." [41] Cabala deals with

the immortality of the soul, the angels, the Supreme Founder of all things, the Cause of Causes, who created the heavens and the earth, the word, and the Holy Ghost, the merit and beatitude of the just, and, finally, the damnation and the punishment of the impious and the transgressors of divine law.[42]

In closing the first chapter Montecuccolus lauds Pico for bringing its principles to light.[43]

In the second chapter Pico's division into *sephiroth* and "nomina divina" is quoted.[44] The study of the *sephiroth* is declared to be the "true cabala" and to work "for the growth of the Catholic faith and the greater confusion of the Jews of this age." [45] The doctrine of the *sephiroth* is then explained in terms of the aphorism from *Pirke aboth*, "By ten words the world was created." [46]

The third chapter of the work of Montecuccolus briefly explains the concept of *Adam kadmon*, the archetypal man. It is more notable, however, for its equation of the triad of the first three *sephiroth*,

---

[40] See Herford, ed., *Pirke aboth*, p. 19.
[41] Montecuccolus, *In cabalam*, p. 20.   [42] *Ibid.*, p. 18.
[43] *Ibid.*, p. 21. Pico is referred to as "lumen Italiae nostrae Picus Mirandulensis."
[44] *Ibid.*   [45] *Ibid.*, p. 23.
[46] *Ibid.*, pp. 23–24. Herford, *Pirke aboth*, p. 124, translates this passage "By ten *sayings* the world was created." This is more faithful to the Rabbinic tradition. It is easy to understand, however, how Montecuccolus derived his variant translation and thence his interpretation.

"Cheder" (*keter*), "Cocma" (*chochmah*), and "Bina" (*binah*), with the first, second, and third persons of the Trinity,[47] an interpretation which is common in the tradition stemming from Pico.

The doctrine of the four worlds, as stated by Montecuccolus in his fifth chapter, makes *aziluth* the world of the *sephiroth; beriah,* the world of the archangels; *yetzirah,* the world of the angels; and *asiyah,* the world of the creation of the heavens, of the heavenly spheres and luminaries, and of the four elements.[48] After this fifth chapter the little book is devoted to exhortation and has no further interest for us.

Besides the writers mentioned here, there were many others whose work was more or less influenced by Pico's cabalistic ideas. These will be dealt with in other parts of the study. It has been my purpose here to show the influence of Pico working as a ferment among many different types of writers. We have met a Franciscan zealot, a Franciscan who was a poetical philosopher, a theologian of note, a leading humanist, a student of esoteric thought, an academic philosopher, and a precocious child who died too young to be classified. All these, from their different places, found in Pico's writings, which seem to us of little significance, the source and in some cases the inspiration of their work.

Pico brought the cabala into the Christian world; largely through his influence it remained a factor in the thought of many people for nearly two centuries. His own knowledge was limited; his overdependence on one source perhaps reprehensible. But the knowledge of others increased because of his limited knowledge; and other sources were studied because he had studied one source. Out of the ashes of "the Phoenix of his age" grew the Christian cabala.

---

[47] Montecuccolus, *In cabalam,* pp. 25–26.   [48] *Ibid.,* p. 30.

IV

PYTHAGORAS REDIVIVUS

ONE HUNDRED YEARS after John Reuchlin (1455–1522) had done his work the impress he had left on European scholarship and the direction in which he had led European thought were so definite that he was referred to as "Rabbi Capnion." [1] In sober truth, this epithet was well deserved, for his services to the cause of Hebrew literature were far greater than were those of many an officially consecrated rabbi.

In our view his two cabalistic dialogues seem of less importance than his professorship of Hebrew, his Hebrew grammar, and the prolonged contest for the preservation of the Talmud which he waged against the bigotry and ignorance of the Cologne Dominicans and the virulence and vindictiveness of the converted Jew, Pfefferkorn. To Capnion himself, however, all these contributions were phases of his interest in the cabala, into which he had been initiated by the Christian, Pico della Mirandola, and the Jews, Obadiah Sforno and Jacob Loans.[2]

Before Reuchlin's study either of cabala or of Hebrew had progressed very far, he wrote a dialogue presenting a Christian interpretation of cabala called *On the Wonder-Working Word*.[3] It is a conventional example of this literary form. It represents a discussion among three men—Sidonius, an Epicurean, Baruch, a Jew, and Capnion, a Christian. Each book of the dialogue represents the conversation of one day. There is a protodramatic quality about these dialogues; the dramatic element is the shifting of the center

---

[1] Marius, *Commentariorum in universam Sanctam Scripturam*, I, 433.
[2] Abrahams, *Jewish Life in the Middle Ages*, pp. 420–21. A full discussion of the Pfefferkorn controversy is to be found in Graetz, *History of the Jews*, IV, 451–507.
[3] *De verbo mirifico libri iii*, first edition Basle, 1494. The dialogue was frequently reprinted. Citations here are from the printing in Pistorius, *Artis cabalisticae . . . scriptores*, pp. 873–979.

of interest from participant to participant. Thus Sidonius dominates the scene in the first book of Reuchlin's dialogue. His antagonist is Baruch whose interpolations on the first night of the discussion determine the character of the discussion of the second night.

In the second phase of the dialogue Baruch predominates. On the third night Capnion, most of whose previous comment has been devoted to mollifying the troubled antagonists by praising both of them, takes the center of the stage for a smashing finale in which he presents the Christian point of view as the answer to both previous positions and in some ways as the resolution of their differences. At the conclusion of the discussion the others accept his point of view.

Reuchlin's Preface summarizes the dialogue thus:

Sidonius, who was at first considered to be of the school of Epicurus, and later found to have sworn by the words of no man, a seeker of wisdom on every hand, in his desire for learning takes a trip in foreign parts. Finally entering Suevia, he meets, in the town of Pforzheim, two philosophers, Baruch, a Jew, and Capnion, a Christian; with them he discusses various fields of thought, and then talks about the knowledge of human and divine affairs; faith, miracles, the power of words and figures, secret rites, and the mysteries of seals. In this way, they examine the holy names and sacred characters of all those peoples who have an eminent philosophy, or who have more refined ceremonies. A careful enumeration of symbols is made by each in behalf of the ritual of his own sect, until finally, in the third book, Capnion brings together from all the sacred names one name to which the virtue and power of all is reduced, which is blessed always, and above all others, IHSVH.[4]

In the first book Sidonius develops an eclectic philosophy largely derived from Epicureanism. In the second book cabalism is first touched upon; the book opens with a request from Sidonius that Capnion tell about the wonder-working word; he does not, however, give Capnion a chance to begin. Instead, he continues talking about his own experiences with all forms of magic and announces his decision that the magic arts are dangerous and vain. After this sweeping denunciation he again expresses his willingness to hear what Capnion has to say on the subject.[5]

---

[4] *De verbo mirifico*, p. 875.   [5] *Ibid.*, II. i, pp. 905–7.

Capnion praises Sidonius for his knowledge and his modesty. He tells of the division of miracles under three heads: physical, astrological, and magical. Those who proclaim this division make astrology dependent upon physics, and magic dependent upon both astrology and physics. This, he says, is foolish; and after an invocation he defends his point of view by the assertion that all miracles may be referred directly to the word and will of God either as exerted by Himself or as delegated to others.[6]

What! exclaims Sidonius, have I spent almost the whole night lying awake in anticipation of hearing the wonder-working word, and do you now calmly about-face and tell me that men can't work miracles? Nonsense! All our lives we've been hearing, on the authority of both sacred and profane historians, that miracles are done by men. Why, only yesterday you said so yourself.[7]

Baruch claims that Sidonius didn't understand what Capnion was talking about; he quotes a number of authorities to support Capnion's contention that miracles are performed only by the agency of God. He is still, however, perplexed about that wonder-working word. Capnion praises Baruch's understanding and asks him whether there are no sacred names in Hebrew.[8]

Baruch begins his discourse by saying that just as heat is essential to the digestive process, the word is necessary to the performance of miracles. We do not know the complete course of digestion; neither do we know the complete process by which God performs miracles by human agency.[9] We do know that the word must be in Hebrew, for that is the oldest language, and it was in Hebrew, as we know from the Bible, that God spoke with men, and men with the angels. "The language of the Hebrews is simple, pure, uncorrupted, holy, terse, and vigorous. In it, God spoke with men and men with angels, directly, face to face, and not through interpreters . . . like friend speaking with friend."[10] He continues by bringing forward classical authorities for the antiquity of the Hebrew tongue and proposes the question whether the Egyptians

[6] *Ibid.*, II. ii–iii, pp. 907–10.   [7] *Ibid.*, II. iv, pp. 910–11.
[8] *Ibid.*, II. v, pp. 911–12.   [9] *Ibid.*, II. vi, pp. 912–14.
[10] *Ibid.*, p. 914.

or the Hebrews first taught the form of letters, that is, had the
earliest written language. His answer is that the Hebrews were the
first to have a written language and that Moses was the first author.[11]

There is only one true God, that of the Hebrews; all others are
daemones. The names of the one true God are more sacred than
those of the other gods. "Therefore, the holy names of the Hebrews are more sacred than those of the Egyptians, both because
they are older, and because they apply to the worship of the one and
supreme God." [12] In the rituals of peoples as diverse as the Brah-
mans of India and the Druids (not to speak of many intermediate
groups of whom Baruch does speak) there are traditional mystic
words of which the people do not know the meaning. These words
are derived from Hebrew sacred words, mispronounced.[13] Sidonius
interrupts to say that while he agrees in general with what Baruch
has said, he feels certain that other peoples besides the Hebrews
have truly sacred names.[14]

This leads Baruch to point out that there are various degrees of
meaning for the word *sacrum*. For his part, he believes the true
meaning to be those things in which God himself has a hand, "not
angels nor demons, but God Himself, the Highest, the Best, the
Greatest." [15] Now, while it is true that other nations have some
share in inspiration, the Hebrew people have more than any other.
Therefore it seems to him that no other people can have sacred
names as effective as those of the Hebrews.[16]

He points out that the evangelist, writing in Greek, took the
Hebrew phrase *Hoshia-na*, meaning "Save, we beseech thee," and
made it *Osanna*, which has no meaning at all. Similarly, the phrase
Thabithi, kumi, which meant "Look back, arise," has been trans-
formed into *Thalita Kumi*, of which at least the first part is mean-
ingless. Other examples of the same type are given. "But," says
Baruch, "while I am trying to find out such Hebrew words as the
evangelists used unchanged in writing, I do not know in what way
I have descended into the mysteries of your religion." [17]

11 *Ibid.*, II. vii, pp. 914–15.
13 *Ibid.*, II. viii, pp. 915–18.
15 *Ibid.*, p. 919.
17 *Ibid.*, p. 923.
12 *Ibid.*, p. 916.
14 *Ibid.*, II. ix, pp. 918–19.
16 *Ibid.*, II. x, pp. 919–20.

Sidonius and Capnion both admire the erudition Baruch has revealed. Capnion begs Baruch to continue; but first Baruch asks about the word *Amen*, which Capnion explains as a token of submission to the will of God, "for all that God wished, he created, both in heaven and on earth." [18]

No one, Baruch continues, knows God and His thought, unless he has the spirit of God within him. Such men know the name of God, and by it they are given power, for by the name of God miracles, signs, portents, and wonders are executed. So he proposes to talk of the various names of God.[19]

There are many names of God. Jerome says there are ten; Dionysius the Areopagite says forty-five; some say seventy-two; others more, and others less. We cannot know exactly, because we know so little about God. Before the sin of Adam, He had only one name; after the fall, one of the punishments of mankind was to lose the one name and to fall among a multiplicity of other names. But Zechariah says, "On that day the Lord shall be one, and His name one," [20] so there is still hope.[21]

Of the many names, some are on a higher plane than the rest; these Baruch is going to examine. The first is to be a name which shows the essence of God, which is separation from things, being shut up within Himself. This idea of separation as the essence of God, Baruch claims to have derived from "a noble philosopher of our age," [22] by which title he refers to Pico. The first name is that by which God revealed himself to the people of Israel in the wilderness, *Ehieh* (I shall be).[23]

Then Baruch proceeds to discuss the name *Hu* (He), derived from the verse "I am the Lord, *Hu* is my name; and my glory will I not give to another." [24] This name was represented in Greek by *Tauton*; in Latin by *Idem*, a name which Virgil ascribes to Jupiter. *Hu* is the name under which God does, permits, or denies anything.

---

[18] *Ibid.*, p. 924. [19] *Ibid.*, II. xiii, pp. 924–25.
[20] *Zechariah* 14:9. [21] *De verbo mirifico*, II. xiv, pp. 925–26.
[22] *Ibid.*, p. 926; cf. Pico, *Opera*, I, 23–24.
[23] *De verbo mirifico*, II. xv, pp. 926–27.
[24] *Isaiah* 13:8. The usual translation is "I am the Lord: that is my name." Mistranslation is, however, one of the minor sins of the cabalists. When one is looking for such opportunities as this verse provides, the opportunities make themselves.

It is to this name that we ascribe all the negative attributes. Another divine name is *Esh* (fire), which is universal in all religions. Of the three names so far discussed, *Hu* is the most important; *Esh*, the least.[25]

Capnion says he thoroughly approves of the order in which Baruch has placed these three names, although it is contrary to the opinion of most theologians. In the order *Hu, Ehieh, Esh*, he feels it best represents the ineffable Trinity.

When Capnion speaks of the Trinity, Sidonius rushes in to offer the trinity of major Greek gods, Zeus, the supreme ruler, Athena, goddess of wisdom, and Aphrodite, goddess of love.[26]

Then Baruch asserts that it is only the supreme essence of God which is comprehended by the three names *Hu, Ehieh*, and *Esh*. Below this supreme essence are the ten *sephiroth* or attributes of which the highest is *keter* (the crown); then *chochmah* (wisdom); then *binah* (intelligence). The first is the abyss of inaccessible divinity, the ocean of majesty and of infinite power over all things, both those which are and those which are not. The world was created by *chochmah* and *binah*. The fourth attribute is *netzach* (victory); the fifth, *hod* (honor); then, in the center of the *sephiroth* comes *tifereth* (glory). The seventh attribute is *geburah* (strength); the eighth, *malchuth* (kingdom); the ninth, *chesed* (mercy); and the last, *pachad* (fear).[27]

Apparently Reuchlin, at the time that he wrote this dialogue, had not progressed very far in his cabalistic studies. He saw that a discussion of cabala required an exposition of the *sephiroth*; in this respect he may be considered to have progressed beyond Pico; he was, however, unable to give their names correctly, nor could he list them in their proper order. He omitted entirely the ninth of the *sephiroth, yesod* (foundation); *geburah* and *pachad*, which are variant names for the fifth *sephirah*, are listed separately as the seventh and the tenth; *chesed*, which should be the fourth *sephirah*, is treated as the ninth; *malchuth*, the tenth, is presented as the eighth.[28]

---

[25] *De verbo mirifico*, II. xvi, pp. 927–29.
[26] *Ibid.*, II. xvii, pp. 929–30.   [27] *Ibid.*, II. xviii, pp. 930–33.
[28] The differences between the correct listing of the *sephiroth* and Reuchlin's listing

Baruch continues by saying that when we want to express God in all these attributes in one word, we use the plural, *Elohim*. But there is another word to express the Essence. This name, in which the highest magical powers known to the Jews are centered, is only half known. The consonants, *Yhvh*, are generally known; the vowels are revealed to only a few. This is the name called the Tetragrammaton.[29]

Capnion asks whether the fact that God had to define Himself to Moses did not mean that He had been forgotten. Baruch replies that God reveals Himself by the name *Yhvh* only to those by whose agency He wishes to perform miracles, and of these Moses was one.[30] He then rhapsodizes about the miracle-working powers of the Tetragrammaton and quotes a hymn of seventy-two verses in each of which *Yhvh* occurs.[31]

Sidonius then shows how many "fours" he can remember; among others, he names the Pythagorean tetractys. Baruch adds more and draws the conclusion that four is a most ancient symbol of mystery.[32]

---

will be instantly clear from the schema below. The Hebrew listing is preserved in order to clarify references to the right or the left column; in reading, therefore, the eye should pass from right to left.

Correct Form

(1) KETER

(3) BINAH		(2) CHOCHMAH	
(5) GEBURAH (or PACHAD)		(4) CHESED	
	(6) TIPHERETH		
(8) HOD		(7) NETZAH	
	(9) YESOD		
	(10) MALCHUTH		

Reuchlin's List

(1) KETER

(3) BINAH		(2) CHOCHMAH	
(5) HOD		(4) NETZAH	
	(6) TIPHERETH		
(8) MALCHUTH		(7) GEBURAH	
	(9) CHESED		
	(10) PACHAD		

[29] *De verbo mirifico*, II. xix, pp. 933–34.
[30] *Ibid.*, II. xx, erroneously numbered xviii, pp. 935–37.
[31] *Ibid.*, II. xxi, erroneously numbered xix, pp. 937–40.
[32] *Ibid.*, II. xxii, erroneously numbered xx, pp. 940–41.

Then Baruch takes the individual letters of the Tetragrammaton and engages in the explanation of their numerical significance; after this he declares that many lesser names of God have not been mentioned: *Ish, Yah, Zevaoth, Adonai, El, Shaddai, Chinon, Elion, Makom, Caphu;* neither the classes of angels nor the names of individual angels have been discussed. These explanations of sacred names must, however, be deferred because of the lateness of the hour.[33]

When the three philosophers get together on the third day, Sidonius and Baruch exhort Capnion to fulfill his promise and reveal the wonder-working word.[34] The word, Capnion explains, is what the Greeks refer to as *Logos,* at once word and reason. The Gospel of John tells us that this was the first created thing and that it was God. But God is the Creator, Cause, and Ruler of all things; the Logos, therefore, is the Son of God.[35]

The Son is "in the bosom of his Father"; this means that he is eternal and coexistent with the Father. Furthermore, the Only Begotten Son is identical in appearance with the Father, so that knowledge of the Son is knowledge of the Father. The name of this Son is *Yhsvh,* Jesus Christ.[36] Three were the miracles in connection with his birth: a virgin conceived and bore a child, and the child was like both God and man. Three are the states in the Word: it is God, it is Son, it is incarnate.[37] The Son is entitled to the attribute *keter,* which Baruch mentioned earlier. There are many manifestations of the Trinity in the Scriptures, from creation on.[38] Those attributes, which are actually of God, are the attributes of God the Father; those ascribed to God because of likeness are the attributes of the Son.[39]

After much suspense Capnion finally avows that the name of the Son is the wonder-working word toward which the entire discussion has pointed. His name is not the Tetragrammaton *Yhvh,* but the Pentagrammaton, *Yhsvh.* The added letter, *shin,* is the determinant element in the word *esh* (fire). Thus the peoples who worshiped

[33] *Ibid.,* II. xxiii, erroneously numbered xxi, pp. 942–46.
[34] *Ibid.,* III. i, p. 947.   [35] *Ibid.,* III. ii, pp. 947–49.
[36] *Ibid.,* III. iii, pp. 949–51.   [37] *Ibid.,* III. iv, pp. 951–53.
[38] *Ibid.,* III. v–vi, pp. 953–56.   [39] *Ibid.,* III. vii, pp. 956–58.

fire approached the truth. Other alphabetical devices show the value of the added letter.[40]

Many instances of miracles performed by the use of the name *Yhsvh* are adduced from the New Testament and the Patristic writings. In particular, Capnion discusses the miracles performed by St. Paul in the course of his wanderings and the miracles of John the Evangelist.[41] He adds that just as the names of Father and Son are alike save for one consonant, so only one element distinguishes the Son from the Father, the son's humanity.[42] The name was revealed in three letters, *Sdy-Shaddai*, in the time of nature; four letters, *Yhvh*, in the time of law; and five letters, *Yhsvh*, in the time of grace. As a name of five letters it partakes of all the virtues of the number five.[43]

Finally, Capnion claims to have proved by Pythagoras and the cabala as well as by Christian authority that the name Jesus is the wonder-working word. He asks both Baruch and Sidonius whether they are not converted by his reasoning. They both accede, far too readily.[44]

It is unfortunate that estimates of Reuchlin as a cabalist should be based upon this book, because it reveals him as a beginner rushing to print. Yet this is the book that is used to define Reuchlin's concept of cabala. Actually, it seems that, even in this book, Pythagoreanism looms larger than cabalism. But it is a pleasant little dialogue, though it proves nothing.

By the time of Reuchlin's second cabalistic dialogue, *On the Cabalistic Art*,[45] the author had really learned Hebrew. He had, in fact, become the leading Christian Hebraist of his age. He had published a Hebrew grammar which, however inadequate, was the first to be composed by a non-Jew. He had read much more widely in the cabala, although he placed far too much emphasis on the work of one author, Joseph ben Abraham Gikatilia. He had become involved in controversy with the Cologne Dominicans over the

[40] *Ibid.*, III. xv–xvi, pp. 970–74.
[41] *Ibid.*, III. xvii–xviii, pp. 974–77.
[42] *Ibid.*, p. 977.
[43] *Ibid.*, pp. 977–78.
[44] *Ibid.*, III. xx, pp. 978–79.
[45] *De arte cabalistica libri iii*, in Pistorius, *Artis cabalisticae . . . scriptores*, pp. 609–730.

Talmud; in fact, he wrote his second cabalistic dialogue as a form of special pleading for the protection of Hebrew books because of their "Christian" content.

As in the earlier dialogue, there are three participants: Philolaus Junior, a Pythagorean, Marranus, a Mohammedan, and Simon of Frankfort, a Jewish cabalist. The dialogue opens when Marranus and Philolaus, who have been eating dinner at the same inn, get acquainted and discuss the fame of Frankfort as a center of cabalistic studies. Philolaus has come from Thrace to discuss cabala with Simon ben Eliezer, who is described as a descendant of R. Simon ben Yochai. This description may have been meant literally by Reuchlin, or it may mean "a noted cabalist."

Marranus asks permission to accompany Philolaus on his visit to Simon so that he may learn more about Pythagoreanism, which is not well known in his part of the world, where all the philosophers are peripatetics. When Philolaus starts to tell him all about Pythagoreanism, Marranus insists that he wants to hear a discussion, not an exposition.

They meet Simon and introduce themselves. Philolaus explains that Simon's reputation has reached him from Jews who were exiled from Spain in 1492. Simon explains that he finds a relief from the buffetings of fortune in the deep study of cabala. When asked to explain cabala, he begins by telling about creation's having taken place by the power in the name *Adonai*, and refers this to the second chapter of Gikatilia's *Porta lucis*.[46]

Next, basing his statement on a passage in the book called *Ruah hen* (*The Spirit of Grace*),[47] Reuchlin asserts in the character of Simon that there are four different classes of mixture of the four elements:

Since, in this sensible world any *murcab*, that is, mixture, is composed of the four elements, it either entirely lacks the soul which would produce a diversified motion, lying immobile and quiescent, like stone and iron; or it grows and increases, like plants and herbs; or it is moved around

---

[46] Joseph ibn Gikatilia, *Sha'are orah* (*The Gates of Light*), p. 21*v*.

[47] The authorship of *Ruah hen* is usually attributed to R. Judah ibn Tibbon. Recent opinion inclines to the belief that it is really the work of R. Jacob Anatoli; see "Introduction," pp. 4–8.

in many places, progresses and lives as much as brute beast and shellfish; or it even speaks rationally, like man. Our youths are accustomed to learn this from the book *Ruah hen*, that is, the spirit of grace, by these Hebrew names: *hadomem, hatzomeh, hahai, vehamedaber*, that is, the dormant, the productive, the living, and the speaking.[48]

Simon goes on to mention the relation of the practical cabala to alchemy, but he maintains that it is a sublimated form of alchemy. "Thus we consider as lurid and sordid and low with dirtiness those things which are said to be in the lower world, and we admire as pure and notable and adorned with unbelievable beauty and we praise highly those things which are said to be in the upper world."[49] Cabala is a way of transforming external perceptions into internal perceptions; these into imagination; this into opinion; opinion into reason; reason into intelligence; intelligence into mind; and mind into light which illuminates mankind. For this reason, the cabalists place light in the center of the "tree of ten numerations," the *sephiroth*, in that one called *tifereth*, or glory.

Simon goes on to describe the relation of the *sephiroth* to *Adam kadmon*, the primordial man. He tells of the marvelous economy of the creation of man: his feet on the ground; his head in the sky; his hands between, so that they can stoop to earth or rise to the sky; eyes so placed that they can look at the earth for the good of the body or at the sky for the good of the soul. Thus designed, man is the microcosm.

We arrive at knowledge of God by way of moral, natural, and mathematical truths. The necessity for ten *sephiroth* is explained on the basis of *Sefer Yetzirah*.[50] The supreme form, fire, is represented in man by the intellective soul. Man must live a temperate physical life, because intemperance destroys the desire to study. These are examples of moral and natural truths. Next we come to the great value of mathematics to the cabalist. Simon insists that the cabalists are following Aristotle in their preoccupation with mathematics, for, as Abubacher asserts, Aristotle's lack of concern with mathematics was due only to the fact that mathematics had not been perfected in

[48] Reuchlin, *De arte cabalistica*, p. 614; see *Ruah hen*, pp. ½–4.
[49] *De arte cabalistica*, p. 615.
[50] See *Sefer Yetzirah* (*The Book of Formation*), pp. 21–23.

his day. That is, Simon understood Abubacher to mean that Aristotle's thinking betrays a mathematical mind.

The word "cabala" is explained by reference to the Hebrew root *kbl*, meaning to receive, that is, to hear and to accept. God cannot, however, be confined in a syllogism. "To explain the merit of creation to flesh and blood is impossible."[51] If this is true of creation, which is natural science, how much more so is it true of the *merkavah*, which is spiritual science. The only way to discuss divine matters is by inference from the mundane.[52] Cabala is a divine revelation. Those who received the revelation directly are called *cabalici*, their pupils, *cabalei*, their imitators, *cabalistae*. Cabala is above dependence upon sense perceptions and not subject to the rules of logic. It is a technique for achieving salvation.

The cabalistic method of expounding the allegorical sense of the Scriptures recognizes that no part of the revelation, however minute, can be vain.

Moreover, by order of the Supreme God, this [cabala] shows him the way of atonement, and cabalistically he expounds the Divine word, taken in an allegorical sense, in which not merely not a single word, but not even a letter, however small and scant, and not even an ornament is placed in vain.[53]

Simon reasons from the fact that God said to the angels, "Behold Adam, just like one of us," that there was a celestial Adam who assumed earthly qualities at the fall. Onkelos, he says parenthetically and without foundation, inaccurately interpreted this remark to mean "Behold Adam was my only begotten son." When Adam fell, God sent the angel Raziel to reveal the Tetragrammaton to him. This revelation was the beginning of the cabala. From this remote time Simon carries the history of the cabala down through the ages to his own day, making reference to Pico as the originator of Christian studies in the cabala.

There follows [54] a list of sources of cabalistic knowledge, from which Archangelus of Borgo Nuovo derived the list which has already been mentioned in connection with his *Apology*. The stric-

---

[51] *De arte cabalistica*, p. 620.　　[52] *Ibid.*
[53] *Ibid.*, p. 622.　　[54] *Ibid.*, pp. 628–29.

tures which were applied to that list apply equally to the list compiled by Reuchlin.

After he has repeated the distinction between "opus Bereshith," natural philosophy and "opus Mercava," spiritual science, Simon continues by explaining that there is agreement between the cabalists and Talmudists on the existence of two worlds, *olam haba*, the intellectual world, and *olam haze*, the sensible world. The Talmudists are concerned with the sensible world; the cabalists have transferred their attention entirely to the intellectual world. It would seem that Reuchlin was here engaged in a form of special pleading; one year earlier he had defended the Talmud; now he seems to be saying, "Destroy the Talmud, which is concerned with the sensible world, if you must; but do not destroy the higher truth, the cabala, whose concern is the intellectual world, and whose value to Christianity I am about to reveal to you."

On this basis, too, can be explained what otherwise must be attributed to ignorance, Reuchlin's inclusion of noncabalistic works in the list of sources referred to earlier. He realized that there was little hope for books branded as Talmudic; he tried, therefore, to save as many Hebrew books as possible by calling them cabalistic and winning papal support for cabala. *De arte cabalistica* was, after all, dedicated to Pope Leo X, one of the Medici, the same pope who expressed himself as "greatly pleased" when he received the dedication of Erasmus's new Latin version of the Scriptures, a work by no means favorable to the Church position. Reuchlin did not have the subtlety of Erasmus; as we shall see, he made open reference to his part in the Battle of Books. He was, however, quite sagacious enough to attempt to get the pope on his side and on the side of the books he listed.

Simon then goes on to interpret "In the beginning God created the heavens and the earth" as the creation of form and matter. There are, he says, two worlds, "corporeal and incorporeal, visible and invisible, sensible and intellectual, material and ideal, a lower world and a higher world." [55] For this reason the Hebrew Scriptures begin with the letter *beth*, the second letter of the Hebrew alphabet,

[55] *Ibid.*, p. 633.

representing the number two and introducing a dualism of worlds.
He quotes Gikatilia to the effect that there are two hells, one for the
body in this world, one for the soul in the world to come, and then
quotes Maimonides to prove that there are two heavens.

Next, he discusses the messianic hope of Israel and shows whence
the cabalists derive their belief that the Messiah will work by means
of the Tetragrammaton, *Yhvh*. In the course of this discussion he
quotes Gikatilia repeatedly.

Simon returns to the idea of the microcosm to say that just as
there is matter, form, and spirit in the world, there is a body, mind,
and soul in man. There are, he continues, three words corresponding
to body, mind, and soul. These are the world of body, the world
of intelligences, and the world of God.

God is a principle of unity. "Word and Voice are produced out of
Spirit." [56] These three, Spirit, Word, and Voice, are one, because
God is one. He is the *En Soph*, the first without a beginning and
the last without an end, the Infinite. The imminence of the Sabbath
necessitates ending the day's discussion; the first book concludes,
therefore, with praise of cabala as a study which raises man to the
plane of the angels and makes of man a companion to the angels.

Simon's absence on the Sabbath leaves Philolaus Junior and Marranus to keep the discussion alive through its second day. After
paying long tribute to the ability of Simon, they decide to spend the
day finding Greek authorities for the ideas that Simon has ex-
pounded. Philolaus begins by telling of the travels of Pythagoras;
the extent of his journeyings made him more a Barbarian than a
Greek. He suspects that not only the philosophy of Pythagoras but
also all philosophy sprang from Hebrew sources. [57]

There follows a long proof, chiefly from Aristotle and his commentators, that there is a realm of supernatural things, unknowable
by the processes of reason. Marranus adds supplementary authorities. It is interesting that Marranus, the Mohammedan, quotes the
patristic writings, Philolaus, only the Greeks. This realm of supernatural things is the subject of cabala, and it was Pythagoras who
brought the doctrines of cabala into Greece. [58]

Philolaus explains the number theories of Pythagoras. The num-

[56] *Ibid.*, p. 640.   [57] *Ibid.*, p. 643.   [58] *Ibid.*, p. 649.

ber two is the first of numbers, for one is not a number, but the source of all numbers. Three is the sum of the first of numbers and the source of numbers. Four is the square of the first number and completes a series (1,2,3,4) whose sum is ten. Four is, therefore, the completion of the tetractys. Other meaningful "fours" are discussed and finally referred to the Tetragrammaton.

The messianic ideal presented by Simon is brought into question. Philolaus asks whether Hercules, Esculapius, Decius Brutus, and similar figures of classical antiquity were not messiahs. Marranus replies that the saving they effected has only a temporary and worldly character, whereas the salvation effected by the true Messiah should be eternal and spiritual.

Then Pythagoras is lauded for having introduced the idea of resurrection to the Greeks. Philolaus shows that number is the basis of all Pythagorean symbolism. He develops the numerical implications of two (duality) as the basis of all contrarieties, and of ten as the perfect number. The virtues of the tetractys are elaborated. Marranus marvels at the closeness with which Pythagoras approached the principles of such religions as Mohammedanism and Christianity. His conception of Pythagoreanism is somewhat inclusive, however, for he refers to Plotinus as "that famous Pythagorean," [59] and to Porphyry as "the great explorer of Pythagorean ideas." [60]

Philolaus continues his explanation by pointing out that there must be three essentials in creation: matter, form, and that which brings them together. This third essential is not supplied by Aristotle's concept of privation, because privation is not a motive force. Plato was nearer when he spoke of God, Idea, and Matter, which Pythagoras had expressed earlier as the Infinite (God), the Monad (Form, or Idea), and the Dyad (Matter). Philolaus then proceeds to a brief exposition of the Pythagorean philosophy under the headings "physics," "education," and "politics." At the end of this exposition Marranus concludes the day's discussion by saying in part, "Out of the infinite sea of the cabalists, Pythagoras brought his river into the limits of the fields of the Greeks." [61]

As the third day's discussion opens, with all three participants

[59] *Ibid.*, p. 672; see also, p. 670.   [60] *Ibid.*, p. 682.   [61] *Ibid.*, p. 683.

present, reference is made to the Pfefferkorn controversy, in which
Reuchlin had been entangled. The whole question is dismissed as
"a small and puerile matter." [62] The actual discussion begins with
the Sabbath as its subject; Simon says that according to Gikatilia's
Porta lucis the Sabbath is a mystery of the living God. There are
two Sabbaths: the Sabbath in the eternal world, or the Jubilee, which
is as day compared with the night of the Sabbath in this world.

Here Simon refers to the Latin translations of cabalistic works
which Pico sponsored and to the Latin translation of Gikatilia's
Sha'are orah, which had been completed under the title *Porta lucis*
by "Paul Ricci, once one of us," [63] for Ricci had been converted
from Judaism to Christianity.

Proceeding from the idea of the Jubilee, Simon discusses the fifty
gates of understanding. No man, he says, has ever been master of all
fifty. Moses was master of forty-nine; Solomon, of forty-eight. The
gate which none but God could master was that of vivification. Just
as there are fifty gates, there are fifty years in the Jubilee. So there
are two fifties and ten *sephiroth*. If we multiply fifty by two and by
ten, the product is one thousand, which is the cube of ten, or absolute
perfection. If we continue to multiply (50 times 2 times 10 times
1,000 . . . times nth product), we reach infinity, the *En Soph*,
God.

The fifty gates of understanding were necessary to creation; so
were the thirty-two paths of wisdom. The thirty-two paths are com-
pounded of the ten *sephiroth* and the twenty-two letters of the
Hebrew alphabet.[64]

If to fifty, which is the number of the gates, be added twenty-two,
which is the number of the letters, the sum, seventy-two, represents
the number of the angels, and the number of the names of God. Of
these seventy-two names of God, Moses used seventy to get the
Hebrew people out of Egypt, and of the other two, one went before
the Israelites as a pillar of cloud by day, the other as a pillar of fire
by night. There must be seventy-two names, because seventy-two is
one of the numerical derivatives of the Tetragrammaton.[65]

---

[62] *Ibid.*, p. 684.   [63] *Ibid.*, p. 686.   [64] *Sefer Yetzirah*, p. 21.
[65] This, of course, does not appear from the simple numerical equivalents of the
letters of the Tetragrammaton: ($y = 10$; $h = 5$; $v = 6$). But little difficulties

The seventy-two angels we can name by adding either *Yah* or *El* with an occasional "i" for euphony, to seventy-two groups of three letters produced by an unusual method of reading three verses in Exodus xiv.[66]

Since the number seventy-two has been proved to be a derivative of *Yhvh*, the seventy-two angelic names make up one symbolic name of God. Simon quotes a Hebrew hymn of seventy-two verses, in each of which appears the name *Yhvh*; this is followed by the Latin translation of the hymn which was included also in *De verbo mirifico*.

The *sephiroth* are associated with names of God and are themselves names of God. They are listed correctly here. Reuchlin has apparently learned more about the *sephiroth* than he knew when he wrote his earlier dialogue. He completes the schema by explaining that the *En Soph* is placed above the highest of the *sephiroth*.

Cabalistic interpretations may be made by substituting letters, code-wise, as in Pico's use of the letters *M, Tz, P, Tz* instead of *Y, H, V, H*.[67] This is done by reversing the alphabet, the so-called *atbash* substitutions. Interpretations may also be made by numerical substitutions, that is, by substituting a word of identical numerical equivalence for any word in the Scriptures, as "Metatron" for "Shaddai."[68] The third method of interpretation is arrived at by using each letter of a word as the initial letter of another word and thus expanding the original word into a phrase. For example, the word "Amen" can be expanded into *Adonai Melech Ne'eman* (The Lord is a Righteous King).[69]

These three parts of the cabalistic art are called gematria, or the art of numbers; notarikon, or the art of abbreviation; themura, or the art of changing letters. Hence, the cabalistic art is represented by the abbreviation *gnt*, which is the construct form of the Hebrew

---

of this sort are easily overcome by the cabalistic technique of gematria; the result required can be achieved by treating the letters of the Tetragrammaton thus: y = 10, yh = 15, yhv = 21, yhvh = 26; total, 72.

[66] See Ginsburg, *Kabbalah*, pp. 132–36.   [67] Pico, *Opera*, I, 82.

[68] The numerical values of the letters in the name Metatron total 314, as do those of the name *Shaddai*.

[69] This type of interpretation may also be used in reverse.

word meaning a garden. For example, Gikatilia called one of his books *Genat egoz* (*A Garden of Nuts*).

The word *hvyh*, to be, contains the same letters as the Tetragrammaton; it is, therefore, the same as the Tetragrammaton. There are three names of God included in the Tetragrammaton: *Yhvh*, *Yhv* (which stands for *Ehieh*), and *Yh*, or *Yah*. These are different names, but they all represent the supreme attributes of the Tetragrammaton when used in combination with other names of God.

If to twenty-six, the numerical equivalent of *Yhvh*, be added one, for the unity of God, and four, for the number of letters, the sum, thirty-one, is the numerical equivalent of *El*. If to *El* be added *vh*, the last two letters of the Tetragrammaton, the resulting name is *Elvh*, or *Eloah*. If to *El* be added the first two letters of the Tetragrammaton *yh*, in reverse order, and a grammatical *m*, the result is *Elhym*, or *Elohim*. Such reversal of letters is not unusual in cabala. Thus all these divine names are derivatives of the Tetragrammaton. There are twelve possible combinations of the letters *Yhvh*, all of which are, for cabalistic purposes, treated as one name.[70] The divine name *Shaddai* is composed of the prefix *sh*, meaning "that which," and the root *dai*, meaning "enough." This name of God means, therefore, "the self-sufficient." Simon refers to Baruch, in *De verbo mirifico*, in explanation of the performance of miracles by the use of the name *Yhvh*.

It has been said that the name Maccabee (*Mkby*) stands for the initial letters of the phrase *mi kamocha baelim Yhvh* (Who is like Thee among the mighty, O Lord?). It is also true that the numerical equivalent of *mkb* is seventy-two, and these three letters stand for the seventy-two names of God.[71] *Y* stands for the Tetragrammaton, *Yhvh*.

The name of each Hebrew letter has a meaning. These meanings

[70]
YHHV	VHHY	HHYV	HHVY
YHVH	VHYH	HYHV	HVHY
YVHH	VHHY	HYVH	HVYH

[71] Unfortunately, this argument is not even valid in its own terms, since the numerical equivalent of *mkb* is only sixty-two (mem = 40; kaph = 20; beth = 2). The numerical equivalent of *mkby* is, however, seventy-two (yod = 10), and the version in the text represents Reuchlin's misunderstanding of his source.

are explained by Simon, who gives also the numerical equivalent of each letter. The units represent the realm of angels; the tens, the realm of spheres; the hundreds, the realm of elements. Each letter has a symbolical meaning, representing an angel, a heavenly body, or an element.

The letters *bch* mean "in Thee"; their numerical equivalent is twenty-two, the number of letters in the Hebrew alphabet. So the phrase "I shall exult and rejoice in Thee" may be interpreted as "I shall exult and rejoice *bch*" or "in the alphabet," because the twenty-two letters are the foundations of the world and of the Law. There are two hundred and forty-two combinations of letters in themura. The equivalent of two hundred and forty-two is *brm*, which means "in the Exalted."

The names used in explanation of *Yhvh* contain forty-two letters; the sum of the numerical equivalents of the spelled-out letters of the Tetragrammaton is also 42: *yvd* (10,6,4), *h* (5), *vv* (6,6), *h* (5). From the Tetragrammaton flows the twelve-letter name *Ab Ben Veruach Hakadosh*, Father, Son, and Holy Spirit. From this flows the forty-two letter name *Ab Elohim Ben Elohim Ruach Hakadosh Elohim Shelosha Beachad Achad Beshelosha*, that is, The Father is God, the Son is God, the Holy Spirit is God; Three in One and One in Three.[72]

Marranus suggests that the use of the Cross as a symbol and the expansion of IHSV into "In Hoc Signaculo Vince" proved the universal validity of the cabala. Simon concludes by saying that while this may be true, he has no time to go further into the discussion of cabalistic mysteries, save to say that their purpose is to make it possible for men to die well by living well.

The closing epistle, addressed in Reuchlin's name to Pope Leo X, calls for that dignitary's support against the fanatics in the matter of the burning of the Talmud.

Reuchlin was influenced in his writings largely by Joseph Gikatilia; we know that he was familiar with that author's *Genat egoz* and with his *Sha'are orah*, both in Hebrew and in the Latin version

[72] Although this is often cited as the forty-two-letter name of God, I know of no other place where this statement is put into the mouth of a supposedly Jewish cabalist. See Ginsburg, *Kabbalah*, pp. 138–41.

of the convert, Paul Ricci. He seems to have been familiar with *Sefer Yetzirah,* although much of his apparent use of that book may be at second hand through Gikatilia's *Sha'are orah,* in which the materials of *Sefer Yetzirah* are repeated and expanded. He seems not to have known the Zohar save by name. Karl Christ's study of Reuchlin's library indicates that, judging by that part of the contents of this collection which has been recovered, Reuchlin owned comparatively few cabalistic books beyond those of Gikatilia.[73] There is no indication that he had a copy of the translations from which Pico worked, though, of course, his meeting with Pico suggests the possibility of his having read these translations while he was in Italy.

However, even if he knew nothing but the work of Gikatilia, he was closer than Pico to the high point of cabalistic speculation. For Menahem Recanati, Pico's major source, represented a degenerate form of the zoharic school of thought, while Gikatilia was the last of the prezoharic group of cabalists and reveals none of the excesses of the later zoharists. In his systematization of cabalistic ideas Gikatilia has no equal in his own age, though his work is far eclipsed by that of Moses Cordovero, who elevated the zoharic chaos into a philosophic system in the early sixteenth century.[74]

Reuchlin's influence on Georgius has already been noted, as has his effect upon Archangelus of Borgo Nuovo, some of whose work was described, with only slight exaggeration, by Gerhard Scholem, as mere plagiarism of Reuchlin.[75] His most important direct influence was on Henry Cornelius Agrippa and will be discussed in a later chapter.

It may be said, too, that from Reuchlin's time no writer who touched on cabalism with any thoroughness did so without using him as a source. That the Christian cabala was at all respectable is attributable to the respect in which Reuchlin's work was held. He was, it must be remembered, despite his aberrant belief in the identity of cabalism and Pythagoreanism, a humanist and Hebraist of note.

As Pico had his orthodox opponent in Pedro Garzia, Reuchlin

---

[73] "Die Bibliothek Reuchlins in Pforzheim," in *Zentralblatt für Bibliothekswesen* Beiheft 52 (Leipzig, 1924).

[74] For Cordovero see Appendix A.   [75] Scholem, *Bibliographia cabbalistica.*

had his in Jacob Hoogstraten (d. 1527), whose attack on him appeared in 1519 as part of the Dominican campaign against the Jews. Hoogstraten's book is a compendium of quotations from Reuchlin and attacks on the Jews, which has little interest save that it highlights the distinction between the Dominicans and the Franciscans in respect to cabalism and to mysticism in general.[76]

Karl Vossler pointed out that the Franciscan order under the inspiration of Joachim of Floris (d. c.1207) developed a great interest in number symbolism.[77] With this background it is certainly not surprising that the Franciscans took readily to the cabalistic lore that Pico and Reuchlin drew from their Hebrew sources. Crispus was a Franciscan; Georgius, a Franciscan; Archangelus, a Franciscan; Jean Thenaud, who will be met later as author of a French poem on the cabala, was a very prominent Franciscan.

On the other hand, it was the Dominicans whose inspiration was the rational Thomistic philosophy who attacked Reuchlin and by whom much of the censoring of Hebrew books, including cabalistic books, was done.[78] From the prominence of the Dominicans in this work arose the false suggestion that Pico's last work, attacking astrology and the arcane sciences, was written as his recantation prior to his entering the Dominican order.

Reuchlin appears as a character in another dialogue beside his own early work *On the Wonder-Working Word*. Petrus Galatinus (fl. 1520) uses Reuchlin as his mouthpiece for the presentation of cabalistic ideas in his dialogue *On the Mysteries of Catholic Truth*.[79] Galatinus does not permit the smoke screen of Reuchlin's humanistic name of Capnion, nor does he allow the fame of Reuchlin to overshadow the doctrines of cabalism. His main purpose is to attack the obstinacy of the Jews in their beliefs by quoting their own books; the trinitarian interpretation that Reuchlin gave to much of the cabalistic material is valuable for this purpose. So strong is this motive in

[76] *Destructio cabalae seu cabalistice perfidie ab J. Reuchlin capnione in lucem edite.*
[77] Vossler, *Mediaeval Culture*, I, 150–51.
[78] See Popper, *The Censorship of Hebrew Books*. My own copy of Cordovero, *Pardes rimmonim*, 1591 edition, was read and censored in 1595, according to the manuscript note at the end, by Fra Luigi da Bologna, of the Dominican order.
[79] Galatinus, *De arcanis catholicae veritatis*, 1st ed., 1516; reprinted often thereafter, frequently with Reuchlin, *De arte cabalistica*.

Galatinus that, with the exception of Reuchlin's book, he quotes most frequently the palpably fraudulent *Gale razia,* a hodge-podge of bad cabalism and worse Christianity, later established as the work of Julius Conrad Otto, a convert to Christianity.

Of the many minor writers who drew on Reuchlin, only a few will be discussed here. Most, however, of those who are to be discussed in later chapters depended on Reuchlin for their basic knowledge of cabalism.

Some slight information about the cabala early reached the English court. Giles du Guez, tutor to Princess Mary and librarian to both Henry VII and Henry VIII, compiled, probably in 1532, a little introductory course in French conversation for the use of the princess. The method used is interlinear; as is usual when this method is used, either the English or the French had to suffer. The English suffers. One conversation involved "What it is of the soul in generall and speciall, after philosophy and saint Isydore, by way of dyalogue betwene the Lady Mary and her servant Gyles." In the course of conversation Mary says in excellent French (I give the English version):

Trewly, Gyles, I laude your persuacion, for by that ye have sayde of it I parceyve clerelye that it is nat possyble to declare it; the whiche one may conjecte by that that she doth resemble unto God and to be wyllynge to declare his ymage shalde be wyllyng to do a thyng impossyble, bycause that he is uncomprehensyble.

To which Giles replies, from Reuchlin:

Trewly, madame, ye saye the truthe, neverthelesse that the scripture wytnessed, that Moyses by the graunt of God dyd merit to se his posterioritie, the whiche is to understande his workes, of the whiche knowledge, the cabalystes doth make fyftie gates that they name of intelligence, sayeng that the sayd Moyse had nat but fourty and nyne, bycause that the first is to knowe God from the begynnyng, which is impossyble.[80]

This is not very much, but it is symptomatic of the pervasion of knowledge about cabalism. Its importance as an indication is heightened by the fact that Du Guez presents a relatively obscure point

[80] See Génin, *L'Eclaircissement de la langue française,* pp. 1057–58.

rather than one more superficial; by so doing he hints at greater knowledge than he shows.

Another rather more important trace of Reuchlin is to be found in the work of Everard Digby (fl. 1580). This minor English philosopher was an opponent of the logic of Peter Ramus, over which he entered into controversy with Sir William Temple (1553–1626), provost of Trinity College, Dublin. Digby used cabala as the basis of some of his original philosophical ideas and the basis of his mystical theology was Reuchlin's *De arte cabalistica*.[81]

In 1583 Henry Howard, Earl of Northampton (c.1539–1614), published his *Defensative against the Poyson of Supposed Prophecies*. He included one chapter, the very title of which marks an indebtedness to Reuchlin, for it is called "Of the Cabalists Art." [82] Here he declares that there are two types of the "Arte or Grammer, rather of the Cabalists." The first of these was as a technique for arriving at the

Secret Sence or Mystery of expounding Scriptures, written down by Ezra . . . The first institution thereof, was not to divine of things to come, but to interpret and expounde the letter of the law, where the meaning was ambiguous . . . Another kinde of mystery they had likewise, which consisted either in resolving words of one sentence and letters of one word that were united; or uniting letters of one word, or words of one sentence that were disseuered.[83]

The second of these mysteries seems to have been derived from Reuchlin's description of notarikon. This discussion, however, Northampton has included, not for its own sake, but to differentiate between these valid purposes, "not to divine of things to come," and the use of cabalistic techniques in prophecy. For, he continues, after

---

[81] Digby, *Theoria analytica*, contains his cabalistic ideas; his attack on Temple's Ramist logical theories is to be found in Digby, *De duplici methodo*. His position in English philosophy is detailed by Freudenthal, "Beiträge zur Geschichte der englischen Philosophie," in *Archiv für Geschichte der Philosophie*, IV (1891), 452–77, where significant biographical information is also brought forward, establishing definitely that this is not the Everard Digby of the Gunpowder Plot. See also Remusat, *Histoire de la philosophie en Angleterre*, I, 196, and the *Cambridge History of English Literature*.

[82] Northampton, *Defensative*, pp. 94a–96a.   [83] *Ibid.*, pp. 94a–b.

referring to *Tau* in Ezekiel, and *Alpha* and *Omega* in Revelation, to say:

These figures had their use and sence assigned to them by the holy Ghost . . . but I declaime against the follies of the foolish Iewes of this time, and some other giddy cock-braynes of our own, which by the resolution or transporting of letters, sillables, and sentences, are not ashamed to professe the finding out of secret destinies, that hang over all the States and Kingdoms within Europe.[84]

To conclude this brief picture of the extent of Reuchlin's influence, let us consider a passage from a sermon by the Reverend Henry Smith (1550–c.1595), written about 1590 and liberally misinterpreting its source in Reuchlin's *De verbo mirifico:*

Rabbi Hacadosh proveth by art cabalistical out of many places of Scripture not only that the mother of the Messiah shall be a Virgin, but also that her name shall be Mary. Like as also the same Rabbi Hacadosh proveth by the same art out of many texts of Scripture that the Messiah's name at his coming shall be Jesus.[85]

Whether he was understood or not understood, attacked or defended, represented or misrepresented, Reuchlin determined the course of the Christian interpretation of cabala for a century and a half. Out of his work, out of his attempt to restore the Pythagorean philosophy, arose on the one hand the fantastic fringe, headed by Agrippa, to whom the cabala was an aid in alchemy, astrology, numerology, and, ultimately, theosophy; on the other, the solid study of the cabala which will be found in many of the philologians, grammarians, exegetes, and erudites of the sixteenth and seventeenth centuries. In the hands of Reuchlin, cabalism almost became a Christian philosophy and did become a fruitful source of inspiration to many of his followers.

[84] *Ibid.,* p. 94b.
[85] Henry Smith, "God's Arrow against Atheism and Irreligion," in *Works,* II, 381–82.

V

THE CABALISTIC APOSTATES

DURING the sixteenth and early seventeenth centuries a wave of conversions to Christianity, induced, or at least justified by, cabala swept over the Jews. The movement was so marked that in discussing supposedly Trinitarian passages in the Zohar a nineteenth century convert could assert that "the very fact that so large a number of Kabbalists have from time to time embraced the Christian faith would of itself show that there must be some sort of affinity between the tenets of the respective systems." [1] Not all these converts were ignorant and passionate men like the disciples of the thaumaturgic cabalist Jacob Frank in the eighteenth century. Some of them were highly educated men who later went on to notable careers in the non-Jewish world.

One of the earliest, and certainly the most distinguished, of these cabalistic apostates was Paul Ricci, a prolific writer on many subjects. After his conversion to Christianity, Ricci became physician to Maximilian I, and in 1521, Professor of Greek and Hebrew in the University of Pavia. [2]

Pistorius, in his anthology of Christian cabalistic writers, [3] devotes much space to Ricci, republishing in its entirety his lengthy dialogue *De coelesti agricultura* in four books, and a number of smaller tracts. These shorter tracts were originally published in the second decade of the sixteenth century, and at least one of them, an abridged trans-

---

[1] Ginsburg, *Kabbalah*, p. 143.
[2] Biographical material on Ricci is very scanty. The available information can be found in Adams, *History of the Jews*, p. 286; Bischoff, *Kritische Geschichte der Thalmud Uebersetzung, passim*; Fuerst, *Bibliotheca Judaica*, II, 41; III, 155; Michelsen, *Israel und die Kirche*, p. 87; *Memorie e documenti per la storia dell' Universita di Pavia*, I, 169.
[3] In fact, half of Pistorius, *Artis cabalisticae scriptores*, is devoted to the work of Ricci.

lation of Joseph Gikatilia's *Sha'are orah*, was known to Reuchlin.[4]

The first three books of Ricci's *De coelesti agricultura* seem to form a spiritual autobiography. The first book is largely devoted to an Aristotelian defense of the Apostle's Creed, in which a Brother Gometius provides the theological accompaniment to the discussions and questions of three blood brothers, Philalethes, moving spirit in the investigation of matters of faith; Philosomatus, the stock Epicurean of the time; and Philadelphus, a youngster without definite character. Save for a reference to the ten *sephiroth* and ten paradigmatic names of God [5] in an invocation by Philalethes, the book is not cabalistic. To what extent it is autobiographical cannot, of course, be accurately gauged; it is a portrait, certainly, of that Frater Gometius who in the prologue to Ricci's *Philosophia prophetica* addresses the author as "my spiritual son" [6] and says, "I sincerely hope that this little work of yours will be read by the Jews, for in it they will find that the mystery of Christ is included in the heart of the Law." [7]

Book II of *De coelesti agricultura* is made up of a series of brief tracts. The first of these discusses the problem of the stubborn persistence of the Jews in their ignorance; the second is devoted to quotations from the Old Testament, proving various points of Christian doctrine and culminates in the assertion, based on the Gospels as well as on the Old Testament, that the first coming of the Messiah has taken place and that Jesus was that Messiah. The third tract asserts that the Jew is compelled by the fundamentals of his own faith to admit that every believer in Christ will participate in the kingdom of heaven. This is followed by an appendix, *De legis mutabilitate*, in which Ricci admits that the objection to all his previous statements is that the Law is eternal and immutable. To this objection he presents four points in rebuttal. With the exception of the Decalogue, he says, the Law does not necessarily hold outside the Promised Land and is, therefore, variable, since it is obligatory or not, depending upon place. Secondly, he declares, man, the recipient of the

---

[4] See Reuchlin, *De arte cabalistica*, in which Simon refers to the translation as the work of Paulus Ricius, "quondam noster." Pistorius, *Artis cabalisticae scriptores*, p. 686.

[5] *Ibid.*, p. 14.　　　　　　　　　　　[6] Ricci, *Philosophica prophetica*, p. i.

[7] *Ibid.*, p. 1.

Law, is variable; the Law must therefore be variable. Thirdly, according to the Talmud and Maimonides the Law varies with respect to the time of its application. Finally, according to cabala the Law ceases to operate when the venom of the serpent is removed from man. This is interpreted to mean when man is freed from the burden of original sin by the advent of Jesus.

Book III is a sermon on the text "Fear God and keep his commandments." In this discourse a distinction is made between those who follow the earthly testament and those who follow the heavenly testament; [8] but both are marked for salvation.

Book IV, subtitled *Porta lucis,* is made up of two parts: Ricci's introduction to the cabala and his translation of Gikatilia's *Sha'are orah,* to which reference has already been made. It is thus that the author describes this book in the dedicatory epistle:

Finally, the fourth book fertilizes by means of occult meditations the faithful soul who bears fruit sparsely and rarely, and raises him from these sordid and deficient streams of water to the supernal streams and the eternal spring of living waters, whence he may gather and propagate the fruit of fuller faith and truth.[9]

It is not, however, the supernal streams of living waters with which we are chiefly concerned. For this study, Ricci's introduction is more important than his translation of Gikatilia. This introduction is a closely knit collection of paragraphs, showing a far deeper understanding of the interrelations of the different doctrines of the cabalists than any we have met before. Because of its rarity and because of its systematic presentation of the heart of cabalistic doctrine in brief compass, a complete translation is presented here.

Paul Ricci's Introduction to the Lore of the Cabalists or Allegorizers.[10]

1. That faculty is called cabala which imparts knowledge of human and divine affairs through the allegorical sense of the law of Moses; it is well-named cabala, which means reception, because it is revealed not in writing, but orally; not by argument, but by faith.

[8] Pistorius, *Artis cabalisticae scriptores,* p. 88.   [9] *Ibid.,* pp. 3–4.
[10] This translation is from the text of the second edition, *Pauli Ricii in cabalistarum seu allegorizantium eruditionem isagoge,* Augsburg, 1515.

2. The purpose of the Law, the manner in which it is handed down, and the nature of its adoption show that this [cabala] is a suitable complement to the Law.

3. The purpose of the Law is to adhere more easily and more closely to the Most High.

4. No one adheres easily and closely to the Most High save one who knows Him more easily and closely.

5. He knows God easily and fully (as far as a human can) who understands each of his works with a ready mind.

6. He understands readily who is borne into the very works of God not by the scrutiny of his reason, but by the assertion of firm evidence.

7. The Law ought, therefore, to give faithful testimony concerning each work of the Most High.

8. Since this is not consistent with the literal sense of the Law, it must arise from the cabalistic or allegorical sense alone.

9. Moreover, the manner in which the Law is handed down, which also proves cabalistic knowledge suitable, is prophetic knowledge.

10. Prophetic knowledge is only of those knowables which are in the mind of God or of the angels.

11. What is in the minds of these is asserted to be free from place, time, and any nexus of matter.

12. Divestment from the nexus of matter is not what the literal sense brings forth; however, the Law requires another interpretation, which we call cabalistic, which turns the listener to the words of the true God, and to knowledge of Him.

13. Moreover, the recipient of the Law (whose nature proves this dogma suitable in a third way) is man, who is admitted as microcosm to the image and likeness of God.

14. Whoever is constructed in the likeness of God and as a microcosm, and resembles the Most High and Macrocosm in manner of activity, seeks his own perfection.

15. He resembles (the Most High) because he performs his work by a law like that by means of which the Most High both creates and rules.

16. He creates and rules by an Eternal Law which is implanted in His Eternal Mind.

17. Therefore, just as the microcosm, man, reveals the pattern of the Supreme Creator and Macrocosm, the Law of this microcosm makes known the Eternal Law of the Macrocosm. And since this cannot be dis-

covered in the literal sense, you must acknowledge it to be drawn from the cabalistic or allegorical sense.

18. Cabalistic lore of this sort, although it has lain neglected in recent generations, disordered, and concealed by ancient dust (both because those who pledge themselves adherents of this dogma were curious about trifles,[11] and because its first investigators and writers wished to show youth milk, not food), nevertheless demands of many (I except the leaders of the Church) the utmost of their ability with respect to the Mosaic writings, and we assert that it excels the dogmas of all other philosophers in certainty, in order, in distinction, and in being furnished with power.

19. In certainty, because the mind agrees in it more securely and without fear on account of the height of the divine wisdom of the teacher Moses, with which, as both the number of miracles and the moving testimonies of nature show, nothing false is connected.

20. In order, because it weaves the history of the Law in the same course in which all things are shown to be entirely of human structure; in this Law, indeed, is shown everything known to the human mind: which it carries as far as the very source from which it derives; and soon it returns to the lower world, and fastens the threefold machine together in every part; it turns to the governing of human affairs by a sort of divine oracle, whereby the total happiness of this race is released.

21. In distinction, truly, because it distinguishes duties and ranks through many abstract names which remain unknown to most of the wise.

22. In being furnished with power, moreover, because it enumerates many sacred names to be invoked, and various bodily movements,[12] by means of which we attain more easily and beyond the use of nature to the glories of the Eternal Father and our prerogatives in the lower world, which resemble them.

23. That part of this doctrine which extends the contemplation of knowables by the mind is called theoretical; that part which fits the acquired powers of mind and body to easy contemplation of these and to the performance of human affairs is called practical.

[11] This, judging by the tone of Ricci's system, seems to be an allusion to the Lurianic cabalists' preoccupation with numerology and kindred speculations.

[12] This reference to bodily movements makes it clear that Ricci was familiar with the "prophetic" cabalism of Abraham Abulafia and his disciples; in this occurred the development of posture and breathing as aids to meditation. See Scholem, *Major Trends in Jewish Mysticism*, chap. iv.

24. The theoretical reveals the higher world through the lower world, and, of these, the more hidden through the more known to us.

25. The more known are those which we find in ourselves (I speak of human structures), whence the cabalist says that the Law itself was constructed in the likeness of man.

26. Man whom we call made in the Law reproduces the image of the Threefold Man and of God. I say of the threefold man: one whom we name the supreme and archetypal choir; another whom we see in heaven together with the machinery of the elements; a third whom we perceive made up of blood and bones.

27. Any one of these men (and the Law, too) is divided into masculine and feminine.

28. In the Law, the first law, filling the first four books of the Pentateuch, deals with masculine vicissitudes; the fifth book, which is called Deuteronomy, or the second law, deals with feminine.

29. The sense knows the difference between the male and the female of carnal man by image and operation. Thence we ascend by means of like appearance of actions to the naming of the parts of the other two men and the knowledge of the Most High.

30. Of the great corporeal man, the male is the shining machine of the sky; the female is that which is seen more obscurely in the moon and the elementaries.

31. Of the archetypal man, we say the male is the mental meeting of the angels; the female that which we call animastic.

32. If you observe the male or female of any one of these men by itself, you complete either male or female in nine excellent and perfect members. If, however, you judge the male with the female as one (as these things really are) you will distinguish it to be divided in ten excellent and perfect members, just as both Law and the sacred names of God are.

33. The members of the Law which always remain are the ten indispensable precepts of the Decalogue.

34. So, too, the limbs of carnal man, eternally constituted to be peculiar to himself, are numbered ten, namely: the breath, the brain, the lung, the heart, the liver, the gall, the spleen, the kidneys, the genitals, and the womb, with their interconnections.

35. The ten peculiar members of the great corporeal man are the intellectual heaven, the *primum mobile,* the orb of the stars, Saturn,

Jupiter, Mars, the Sun, Venus, Mercury, and the Moon together with the rest that her sphere includes.

36. The members of the archetypal man are the ten choirs of angels: those nine which the Hebrews call *haios hacodes, offanim, erelim, hasmalim, seraphim, malachim, elohim, bene elohim, cherubim,* and which the sacred school of theologians call: *cherubim, thrones, powers, virtues, dominions, preeminences, archangels, angels.* The tenth, which the cabalists and many of the saints and philosophers place in the animastic (sc. feminine) order, is usually called by its Hebrew name, *iscim,* that is, *men.*

37. Finally, the paradigmatic names of God are ten, grouped together in the form of a denarius: *Ehieh, Ioh, YHVH Elohim, El, Eloha, Elohim, YHVH Zevaos, Elohim Zevaos, Sadaii, Edonaii.*

38. These ten paradigmatic names by hyperbole (just as, also, the other members of the two men by participation) are ten *sephiroth,* that is, *numerations,* and it is right for these to be known by various names, some of which we publish as examples.

39. The first *sephirah, Ehieh, Supreme Diadem,* privation, father, mind.

40. The second, *Ioh,* Wisdom, first-born, essence, unformed.

41. The third, *YHVH Elohim,* Spirit of God, jubilee, the great trumpet, the female who forms, the conversion of the penitent, the redemption of the world, the life of the world to come.

42. The fourth, *El,* Grace, magnificence, the right hand of pity, the waters above.

43. The fifth, *Elohim,* Firmness, judgment, the left hand.

44. The sixth, *Eloha,* Glory, the middle line, pleasure, the tree of life.

45. The seventh, *YHVH Zevaos,* eternity, the right hand column.

46. The eighth, *Elohim Zevaos,* confession, the left hand column.

47. The ninth, *Sadaii,* Foundation, the just, Israel, Joseph, the good intelligence, Sabbath, rest, redemption, the rite of circumcision.

48. The tenth, *Edonaii,* Kingdom, the congregation of Israel, the temple of the King, the bride, the queen of the sky, the virgin of Israel, the gates of God, the kingdom of the house of David, the garden of David. There are many names of this kind which can be seen collected in the following compendium and volume of divine ordinances (called *Maereches elohim*). Finally, the cabalists reduce individual prophetic

utterances to this sephirotic oracle (which I consider worthy of the greatest praise), so that the unlearned, with an ordinary education, not to
speak of the wise, possess the ability to convert universal hagiographic
words from the literal to the allegorical sense.

49. Of the ten paradigmatic *sephiroth*, some correspond with the
essence of the Creator, in itself; others are congruent with the essence,
as related externally to creatures. The three loftier ones, namely, Supreme
Crown, Wisdom and Prudence, are of the first type; the seven remaining are of the other type.

50. The loftier three (the first of which they call father; the second,
first born; the third, spirit of God) are defined as constituting a simple,
coequal unity of essence (as the compiler of the divine ordinances says);
but the other seven stand apart from each other, since these seven are
examples of the gifts of the spirit; because we see them disunited not in
the supernal mind, but in the world of creation. So, for example, we
consider that one of the loftier three examples which refers to the sensi-
tive flesh of a girl to encompass the essence itself.

51. For we know that there is a real distinction between privation,
matter, and form, and yet we judge them to be one with the corporeal
essence of the thing itself. But we perceive body, element, mineral, vege-
table, animal, rational, intellectual, to be set apart from the thing itself.

52. As long as he inhabited the garden of pleasure, the first Adam
knew all these ten *sephiroth* (as Moses Gerundensis, Rabbi Menahem
Racanati, and the volume of divine ordinances declare) by contemplation
of mind, without the dictate of the Law.

53. But when (as is stated in the same places), at the stimulation of
the serpent and Eve, he ate of the tree of knowledge of good and evil,
he did not cut around its skin; he cut off a twig from its proper root,
and he separated Kingdom from Foundation; [13] he was expelled with all
his offspring from the garden of pleasure, and (by dictate of the Law)
he could achieve only seven *sephiroth*.

54. But (as both Rabbi Simon in *Porta lucis* [14] and the compendium
of divine ordinances state) until original sin, or the venom of the serpent
shall have been taken away, he will by no means deserve to contemplate
the highest three.

[13] See Pico, "The sin of Adam was the separation of the kingdom from the other
branches," *Cabalistic Conclusions*, No. 4.
[14] That is, R. Simon ben Yochai is quoted, in Gikatilia's *Porta lucis*, as having
said this.

55. When the venom of the serpent is removed, the Law itself stops; since, as Rabbi Menahem and the ordinances relate, the conversion of the penitent draws near.

56. Indeed the day approaches (as the Law decrees Leviticus, xxx) when every possession reverts to its earliest owner, and every slave returns to his family a free man.

57. The slave returns and the possession reverts, while the reed pipes respond each to each, and the great trumpet of the jubilee resounds.

58. The trumpet of the jubilee resounds when the seven remissions which precede the day of the Great Sabbath of which there is no evening (as Rabbi Simon and Moses Gerundensis, and also the eighth chapter of *Porta lucis* and the compilation of divine ordinances point out) are almost completed; which neither the great Augustine, nor many later, or for that matter earlier astronomers deny.

59. When these things shall have occurred, the Redeemer of the world, son of Joseph, son of David, who was born of a virgin, queen of the skies, the lofty way of approach to the King and the gateway to Paradise, and who endureth death, grants salvation; at length he judges the world in a conflagration of fire; he revives the rising dead; he delivers to eternity the glorious bodies of the saints.

60. As, in this, the summary of the chief theoretical dogmas of the cabalists has been brought to a conclusion, practical knowledge ought to follow.

61. We contend that this, as well as the theoretical, is derived from the purpose of the Law.

62. For the purpose of the Law (namely, to adhere easily and closely to the Most High) demands an easy way not only of handing down but also of receiving, since activity discloses at least as much as the tendency to receive allows.

63. He receives easily who prepares himself easily both inside and out for reception, and who can easily resist obstacles at the gates and inside. For often readiness is allowed by nature and often by knowledge to someone, whom, nevertheless, a lack of provisions, the wicked society of mortals, and the threats of the stars turn aside.

64. Indeed, he resists, and easily prepares himself who adapts himself to times, to places, and to the angelic powers of these, or to the power of Him whom the sacred chorus of theologians determines to be the preserver of men in anything whatsoever; from this point, he is able to come more easily to the Father of lights.

65. He approaches (as the cabalists and the Talmudists, and Rabbi Isaac, the great interpreter of the Book of Creation,[15] avow) through the angel Raziel, who taught Adam himself. Shem, son of Noah, approached through the angel Iosiel; Abram through Zadkiel; Isaac through Raphael; Jacob through Piliel; Joseph through Gabriel; Moses through Metatron; Elijah through Maltiel; and this must also be judged about many others.

66. Therefore complete allegorical knowledge of the cabalists or of the Law extends easily and by a clear succession in the human faculty of knowing to him who prepares his powers of mind and body for easy acceptance; finally, it adapts and joins its cultivator to the Most High, in whom he delights and remains happy to eternity.

The most notable feature of this survey of the cabalistic doctrine is, as has been pointed out, the degree to which the author succeeds in unifying the scattered dogmas. To his orderly mind, cabala was a system, and it is as such that he presents it. In noting this, it is important to state that for the first time in the history of Christian cabalism it was a system which presented a way of life, a definitely mystical path from sense to God for the individual cabalist. In Ricci's system cabala employs the allegorical sense of the Law of Moses to the end that the individual cabalist may associate with the Most High and continue happy to eternity. To Ricci, cabala reveals a possible itinerary of the mind to God.

It is in this feature that the chief distinction between Ricci and his Jewish forbears is made manifest. Jewish mysticism is not a mysticism of individual salvation; it is rooted, not in the life-history of individuals, but in the world-history of the race. Salvation is salvation for all Israel, and in the maturer Jewish thinkers, salvation for all mankind. This is not to suggest that the Jewish mystic did not experience the intense ecstasy of approach to the divine which is the common heritage of mystics of all ages and of all religions. The difference lies in the interpretation of the ecstasies, which is a social or racial interpretation in the Jewish mystics.[16]

Ricci, in his prefaced letter to Doctor Stambler,[17] explains that

[15] Isaac the Blind, one of the founders of medieval cabalism.
[16] Scholem, *Major Trends in Jewish Mysticism*, pp. 21, 388.
[17] Ricci, *In cabalistarum seu allegorizantium eruditionem isagoge*. "Epistola de-

Pico was not a great authority on the cabala; [18] this is obvious when one compares Ricci's systematic treatment with the haphazard aggregation of Pico's conclusions, of which even a favorably disposed writer has said, "To develop any system from these aphorisms would appear almost impossible." [19]

Those elaborate exegetical devices, those toyings with letters and numbers, their permutations and combinations, which were of such paramount importance in the Christian cabala of Reuchlin, do not appear here, nor does the magical application of the numbers, as it does in Agrippa. The alphabetical prestidigitation by means of which *Yhvh* became *Yhsvh* at the conclusion of Reuchlin's *De verbo mirifico* seems pallid before the spiritual flame of Ricci's progress from Adam's original innocence and his knowledge of all ten *sephiroth*, through the Fall and its consequence, the loss of knowledge of the three highest *sephiroth*, to the conversion of the penitent and the redemption of man in the second advent of Jesus, when "the slave returns and the possession reverts, while the reed pipes respond each to each, and the great trumpet of the jubilee resounds."

Among the other Jews who followed the path of cabalism to Christianity was John Stephen Rittangel (1606–1652), who produced the most valuable early Latin translation of *Sefer Yetzirah*.[20] Rittangel was a descendant of the distinguished Jewish thinker and statesman Isaac Abarbanel (1437–1508).

Philip d'Aquines, whose most lasting contribution to the Christian world was a Hebrew dictionary, was also the author of a brief and scarcely noteworthy book on the *Sephirotic Tree*. His interpretations are conventional; he does no more in his entire book than Ricci in ten casual explanatory aphorisms. The piety of latter-day

---

fensoria contra obtrectatorem Cabale ad venerabilem D. Doctorem Stambler," pp. iv–3r.

[18] Apparently someone who had read Ricci's *Isagoge*, either in manuscript or in the first edition, had asserted that he was not writing about cabala, because he had said so much more than had Pico, an amusing example of the stultifying effect of authoritarian thinking. Ricci's reply may be found on p. 2v of the printed version.

[19] Waite, *Kabbalah*, p. 452.

[20] Rittangel, *Liber Jezirah qui Abrahamo patriarchae adscribitur, una cum commentario Rabi Abraham F. D. super 32 semitis sapientia, a quibus liber Jezirah incipit.*

French "cabalists" of the theosophical tradition rescued this work from deserved oblivion by a recent reprint.[21]

Elchanan Paul, in his *Mysterium novum*,[22] follows the trail of Reuchlin to prove by means of the cabala that Jesus was the true Messiah. Paul's cabalistic interpretation was built on a solid basis of familiarity with the Hebrew language, and in his book are some of the better alphabetical tricks of the Christian cabalistic literature.

Joseph de Voisin (c.1610–1685) wrote a brief but excellent account of the cabala as an agent in conversion to Christianity. His apparent purpose was to exclude cabalistic books from the general condemnation of Jewish works in the text to which his account was prefaced.[23]

These and others like them were, however, all men of education. They became, in a sense, missionaries to the Jews, and wrote books defending their Christian interpretations of the cabala. The question immediately arises whether they were followed from the Jewish fold into the Christian communion by any lesser men. This question is, of course, impossible to answer with any degree of certainty, because if there were others, they did not write of their conversion. To this generalization, there is one almost accidental exception.

An ex-Jew named Louis Carretus wrote, in 1553, a letter to his son, in Hebrew, explaining the reason for his conversion and attempting to induce his son to join him. The elder Buxtorf, whose services to the cause of Semitic knowledge were legion, translated this letter into Latin and appended it to one of his works.[24]

Carretus uses many arguments; all, however, are dependent upon the belief that Jesus was the Messiah and was divine. This basic principle is established in the mind of the writer by the already familiar argument that the superior triad of the sephirotic tree, the triad of crown, wisdom, and understanding, represents the Trinity.[25] Jesus, therefore, as the second person of the Trinity, is equated with

[21] Aquinas, *Interprétation de l'arbre de la cabale.*
[22] Paul, *Mysterium novum; ein neu herrlich Beweiss . . . dass der Name Jesus Christus Gottes Sohn . . . in dem fürnehmsten Prophezeiungen von Messia verdeckt bedeutet.*
[23] Voisin, *Observationes.* Prefaced to Raymond Martin, *Pugio fidei. . . .* 1687.
[24] Buxtorf, *Synagoga Iudaica*, pp. 596–644. [25] *Ibid.*, p. 607.

wisdom and with the divine name *Yah* and all its attributes.

Perhaps the Christians who declined to recognize the value of cabala in the conversion of the Jews were less wise than these apostles.
Perhaps they were far wiser, and recognized, as did Mersenne,[26]
that the use of cabalistic interpretations falsified the true appeal of
Christianity. Reuchlin and Pico, in the tradition of Catholic humanism, considered cabala of value; Erasmus and Mersenne (1588–
1648), greater than any of its defenders in the same tradition,
considered it harmful, though Erasmus was tolerant. Pistorius and
Philip Nicolai (1556–1608) [27] in the Protestant tradition were defenders of the cabalistic system. Luther, greater than both in the
same tradition, attacked it.[28]

That mass conversion on a cabalistic basis was possible is proven
by the history of the Shabbetians as well as by the conversion to
Christianity of the 514 followers of Jacob Frank in the eighteenth
century.[29] This conversion, however, may be a historical accident.
Certainly, if cabala could have been used widely as a missionary tool
it is unlikely that the excellent strategists of Christian theology
would have failed to see the value of turning their opponents' own
weapon against them.

[26] Mersenne, *Quaestiones celeberrimae in Genesim cum accurata textus explicatione.*
See also Mersenne, *Observationes et emendationes ad Francisci Georgii Veneti
problemata; in hoc opere, cabala evertitur, editio vulgata et inquisitores sanctae
fidei catholicae ab haereticorum atque politicorum calumniis accurate vindicantur.*
[27] See Lindstrom, *Philipp Nicolais Kristendomstolkning,* chap. iii, which establishes
the partially cabalistic basis of Nicolai's doctrine of creation dependent on the doctrine of love.
[28] See Luther, *Duo fragmenta . . . ad J. Reuchlin De arte cabalistica libros iii.*
[29] See Baron, *History of the Jews,* III, 213, and Graetz, *History of the Jews,* V,
301–5.

VI

THE FANTASTIC CABALA

IN THE sixteenth century magic was well-nigh respectable. Many of the most noted men of the century dabbled in it; to some, as to Marlowe's Doctor Faustus, magic spelled power. The universities did not teach magic, but many of their students practiced it. Magic went far beyond mere formulas of incantation; its doctrines were of far greater import than its practices. Much of the most original thinking of the period is to be found in books on magic.

Among the followers and students of the magical art cabala developed considerable popularity. It became, as it were, a part of the philosophic background required of each member of this fantastic fringe of the intellectual life. It is true that often when the word "cabala" was used the doctrine in no way resembled that of the Hebrew cabala. A. E. Waite pointed out that in the case of Paracelsus "the sole work on the cabala which has been preserved . . . is a short treatise, which forms a detached portion of the book entitled De Pestilitate." [1] This historian of occult movements concedes, however, that this section bears no relation to the Hebrew cabala save in name.

This failure to make the name represent the doctrine is, of course, almost equally true of our contemporaries in the same fantastic tradition who use the word "cabala." It is not long since Wynn Westcott, who should have known what cabala was, asserted that he had taught, in rosicrucian and hermetic societies, cabalistic teachings which had never been published and are not to be found in any Hebrew work. [2] To such occultists as Westcott in our time the actual historic background out of which cabala arose has no meaning and its amplification seems in no sense wrong. Thus, all-too-commonly occult doctrines develop beyond their original patterns.

[1] Paracelsus, *The Hermetic and Alchemical Writings*, ed. by Waite, I, 161*n*.
[2] Westcott, *An Introduction to the Study of the Kabalah*, p. 8.

Some, however, of the sixteenth-century devotees of the magical art actually meant cabala when they used the word, and of these the most distinguished was Henry Cornelius Agrippa of Nettesheim (1486–1535). Agrippa's interest in the cabala was stimulated by Reuchlin, whose *De verbo mirifico* the young occultist studied with great care. As early as 1509 Agrippa delivered a public exposition of Reuchlin's work. His biographer, Henry Morley, explains that by 1509 Agrippa had collected the notes for a complete treatise on magic; some, of course, were from fellow members of secret societies interested in magic, but many "were obtained from Reuchlin's Hebrew-Christian way of using the Cabala." [3] In order to earn the good will of Margaret of Austria, Agrippa decided to apply what he had learned in this close study of Reuchlin's work to a series of public orations on the book in honor of her highness, whom he hoped thus to gain as his patron.

We do not know what Agrippa said about Reuchlin's book. We do know that about a year later, when he was in London on a mission on which he had been sent by the Emperor Maximilian, father of Margaret, and while he was staying at the home of Dean Colet, Agrippa responded in a very mild way to an attack made upon his orations by the monk Johannes Catilinet.[4]

This *Expostulation* was extremely Christian in tone. It was produced at a time when the vicious attacks on Reuchlin by the Cologne Dominicans were in the air, and when the equally vicious but somewhat more toleration-conscious defenses of Reuchlin by Ulrich von Hutten and others [5] were being composed. Yet Agrippa quietly pointed out that he was a Christian, not a "Judaizing heretic," and that the work he defended in public auditory and for whose defense he was rewarded with "a lectureship, the position of Regent, and a salary" was that of "a Christian doctor, John Reuchlin of Pforzheim." His conclusion is that Catilinet must have erred because of a lack of knowledge of cabala and that if given the opportunity to

Morley, *The Life of Henry Cornelius Agrippa*, I, 63.
"Expostulatio . . . cum Iohannes Catilineto," in Agrippa, *Opera*, II, 508–12.
See the scathing *Litterae obscurorum virorum*, which shook Europe with none-too-kind laughter and was largely the work of Von Hutten.

talk with him, Agrippa could change his views. There is no record
of such a conversation having taken place.

Catilinet's attacks were delivered in a series of public orations
before the Princess Margaret at the beginning of Lent in 1510.
Shortly before this, Agrippa had submitted to the Abbot Tritheim
(1462–1516) his work *On Occult Philosophy*. In an accompanying
letter he requested Tritheim's criticism and advice about publishing
his book.[6]

Tritheim kept the messenger while he read the manuscript, and
immediately after completing his reading, April 8, 1510, he sent a
note to Agrippa. He advised Agrippa to continue his occult studies,
but not to publish his book. He wrote: "Speak of things public to
the public, but of things lofty and secret only to the loftiest and the
most private of your friends. Hay to an ox, and sugar to a parrot;
interpret this rightly, lest you be trampled down by oxen as most
others have been."[7] How apt Tritheim's warning against public
presentation of occult ideas was can be seen from the fact that the
attack of Catilinet against Agrippa's lectures followed it so closely.
Agrippa took heed to his friend's advice. This work on occult philosophy was not published until 1531. By this time Reuchlin's *De
arte cabalistica* had appeared, and Agrippa revised his text to include
some material from Reuchlin's better book.

When the work *On Occult Philosophy* appeared, it was divided
into three books. At the beginning of the first book the author asserts
that there are three worlds or realms: the elementary world, the
intellectual world, and the celestial world. This is the schema which
Pico drew from the work of Recanati. The first book deals with the
elementary world, or natural magic. Only at the end does Agrippa
suggest the possibility of magical performance by means of formula
developed from letters, of which, of course, Hebrew letters are most
sacred and effective.

But this you must not be ignorant of, that it is observed by wise men
that the Hebrew letters are the most efficacious of all, because they have
the greatest similitude with the celestials and the world, and that the

[6] Agrippa, *Opera*, II, 702–3; "Epistolarum, Liber I," No. xxiii.
[7] *Ibid.*, II, 704.

tters of the other tongues have not so great an efficacy because they
e more distant from them.[8]

The second book treats of the intellectual world and is chiefly
oncerned with a statement of the symbolism of numbers. Thus we
earn that unity is not a number, but the original of all numbers. We
iscover, too, that as in the celestial world there is but one God,
hose name is written with one letter, so there is in the intellectual
orld one Supreme Intelligence. There are similar treatments of
ie other numbers.

It was this part of Agrippa's book that Friedrich Barth published
a German translation in 1855 as Agrippa's cabala.[9] In Barth's in-
roduction we read that in all oriental languages numbers are ex-
ressed by means of letters and that "the true cabala changes the
etters into numbers, and ascribes to the latter an inner meaning. It
, as it were, the grammar of magic, and bears the same relation to
as the numbers bear to the letters." [10] Barth continues with the
uggestion that men search through the darkest spots of the most
ncient traditions and find there whatever they wish.[11] It is hardly
kely that Barth intended this statement as anything but a compli-
ent to the wisdom and prophetic insight of the formulators of the
ost ancient traditions. It might, however, be taken as a valid com-
ient on the type of research into ancient traditions which produced
he statement by Westcott which was quoted earlier.

Book II may be the true cabala according to Barth; according to
Agrippa it is merely the basis on which the actual cabalistic material
f the third book rests. This third book, which deals with the celes-
ial world, discusses the divine names in a manner thoroughly remi-
iscent of Reuchlin's books.[12] The *sephiroth* are dealt with after this
ashion:

he Mecubales of the Hebrews, the most learned in Divine things, have
eceived the ten principal names of God, as certain Divine powers, or

Ibid., I, 117, from "De occulta philosophia libri tres."
Barth, *Die Cabbala des Heinrich Cornelius Agrippa.*
[9] *Ibid.*, p. 12.   [11] *Ibid.*, p. 16.
[12] A good example is the discussion of the seventy-two-letter name of God, which
pproximates even the wording of Reuchlin, *De arte cabalistica.* For this passage
e Agrippa, *Three Books of Occult Philosophy*, Eng. tr. by J. F., pp. 418–27.

as it were members of God, which by ten numerations which they cal
Sephiroth as it were vestiments, instruments, or examplars of the Arche
type, have an influence on all things created, through the high things
even to the lowest, yet by a certain order.[13]

After this general introduction the *sephiroth* are explained indi
vidually, in great detail. There are signs in this section that th
original form was the erroneous one of Reuchlin's *De verbo mir*
fico, but that improvements have been made on the basis of Reuch
lin's correct listing in his *De arte cabalistica*.

Next we hear of the angels, and finally of the soul:

The soul of man is a certain divine Light, created after the image o
the word, the cause of causes and first example, and the substance o
God, figured by a seal whose Character is the eternal word; also th
soul of man is a certain divine substance, individual and wholly presen
in every part of the body.[14]

The year 1510, so eventful in the career of Agrippa, as we hav
seen, also marked the appearance of his glorification of the femal
sex.[15] This was another of the author's weapons in his attempt t
gain the favor of Princess Margaret. The lady had listened to Cati
linet's attack on Agrippa and the cabala. Agrippa replied to his op
ponent not only directly, in his *Expostulation*, but also indirectly
by writing of the merits of women. In the course of this politica
exercise there is one passage of interest to this study; Agrippa use
the alphabetical technique of the cabalist to prove that there is a
closer correspondence between the name "Eve" and the Tetragram
maton than exists between the name "Adam" and that supreme four
letter name of God.[16]

In 1515 Agrippa fought with the Italians against the French a
the battle of Marignano. As a result of the French victory he wa
reduced to penury. In these straits he was aided by the Marquis o
Montferrat, who was repaid by receiving the dedication of two trea
tises, one on man, the other on the threefold way of knowing God
Only the latter has come down to us.[17] Morley calls it "a longing

---

[13] *Ibid.*, p. 367.   [14] *Ibid.*, p. 465.
[15] Agrippa, *Opera*, II, 518–42, "De nobilitate et praecellentia foeminei sexus."
[16] *Ibid.*, II, 519.   [17] *Ibid.*, II, 480–501, "De triplici ratione cognoscendi deum."

Godward from the depth of suffering, full of an earnest aspiration, with which, however, there had at last come to be joined a bitter scorn of those who, never rising heavenward, pull heaven down to their own sphere, and standing in the churches and monasteries, bar the upward way." [18] Biographers, it is to be presumed, will indulge in rhapsodies.

The treatise is in six chapters; the first of these deals with the necessity for seeking to know God; the second presents the three ways of knowing Him: by contemplation of His creatures, by hearing the angels, and by listening to His Son. The next three chapters discuss these three ways in more detail. The final chapter is a more or less formal summary brought into accord with the creed of the church. In the fourth chapter, dealing with the way of knowing God through angels, Agrippa explains that in addition to the written Law handed down to Moses at Mount Sinai, God revealed to the leader of the children of Israel a complete exposition of the true Law, which is contained hermetically in the written Law. Moses, therefore, received two laws, one literal and one spiritual. In accordance with the precept of the Lord, he communicated the written Law to all the people, the spiritual Law only to the seventy elders. This spiritual Law was handed down by word of mouth from generation to generation. It was, therefore, called "cabala," reception.

Cabala is concerned with those things which may be known about God and His angels. It teaches the many names to be used for the invocation of the angels. The doctrine of the Messiah was a part of the original cabala, but since the Messiah, Jesus, has already come, cabala should now be chiefly concerned with the angels.

At this point Agrippa shows an inkling of the development of an attitude which was later to lead him to renounce all his former pursuits as vanity, when he maintains that cabalists have devoted themselves too much to magic and are thus leading to a misunderstanding of the name and purpose of cabala. Cabala in its true sense is necessary, for if one does not know the technique for looking below the surface of the Scriptures one has only the literal sense to go by. Furthermore, if knowledge is of the literal meaning only, "nothing is

[18] Morley, *Life of Agrippa*, I, 296.

more ridiculous than the Law, or more like old women's fables and mere wanton talk." [19] Since, however, Christ, the sun of all justice, has come, we no longer need this misty and indirect way of knowing God; we can know Him through His Son. God can be known through the Gospels.[20]

In 1526 Agrippa's dissatisfaction with the conditions of his life led to the composition of a remarkable book on *The Uncertainty and Vanity of the Sciences and Arts*,[21] half satire directed against the schools, half renunciation of all his earlier preoccupations. He attacks, in turn, all the sciences and arts and their subdivisions, showing a wide knowledge, for, at some time or other "Agrippa had tried nearly every art that he had found wanting. . . . He was not a reviler from without, but a satirist from within, of the uncertainties and vanities of the imperfect art and science of his day." [22] The treatise closes with an exhortation, largely in the words of the Scriptures, that men should attempt to become like-minded with God; and, learning from Jesus, the true Master, should be wise concerning the good, and simple concerning the evil.

Among his other renunciations is the study of cabala. He describes cabala as an ancient Hebrew tradition, known to Christians for only a short time. It is double science: half treats of cosmology, half of "Marcana,"

which is something of a symbolic theology dealing with sublimer reflections about God, the angelic powers, and sacred names and symbols, in which letters, numbers, figures, things and the names and ornaments of letters, and lines, punctuation, and accents are names significant of most profound things and of great mysteries.[23]

While, he says, there is no doubt that such a secret tradition was handed down to Moses, nevertheless he feels that cabala as practiced by the Jews is a rhapsodical superstition, allied to theurgic magic. If there is a wonder-working name, it is Iesv, which the Jews do not recognize. Cabala is, therefore, now only a vain delusion.[24]

---

[19] Agrippa, *Opera*, II, 489.   [20] *Ibid.*, II, 486–89.
[21] *Ibid.*, II, 1–247, "De incertitudine et vanitate scientiarum et artium atque excellentia verbi dei."
[22] Morley, *Life of Agrippa*, II, 208–9.   [23] Agrippa, *Opera*, II, 68.
[24] *Ibid.*, II, 77–80.

This renunciation did not last; as has been seen, by 1531 Agrippa dared to publish his three books on occult philosophy in their revised form. Thus, for a brief period in his life the skeptic was uppermost in him; both before and after this period he was the credulous philosopher of magic.[25]

Of the successors of Agrippa in the sixteenth century, Paracelsus (1493–1541) undoubtedly is the most important. His name has been associated with Christian cabalism for so long that it is with some degree of shock that one comes to the realization that while the word "cabala" is used by Paracelsus, he had no conception whatsoever of its meaning. The sting of this discovery is, however, mitigated by the recognition that this adept

occupies an exceptional position among occult philosophers; he was not a man who respected or quoted authorities; he owed very little to tradition, very little to what is understood commonly by learning. If we take his alchemical treatises and compare them with Hermetic literature, we shall find that they are quite unlike it, and that he was, in fact, his own alchemist. When he concerns himself with Magic, he has few correspondences which will enable him to be illustrated by other writers on this subject: again, he was his own magician. And as regards the question of the Kabbalah, if we discover, on examination, that he has something to say concerning it, we should expect that it would be quite unlike anything that went before him, and quite foreign to the known lines of Kabbalism. Once more, we should find that he would prove to be his own Kabbalist.[26]

This type of cabalism bears to the work of Reuchlin the same relation that the fantasies of the dreamer bear to waking thought. It justifies fully the title of this chapter.

The few scattered references to cabala in the works of Paracelsus provide a complete basis for Waite's conclusion. In one doubtful reference Paracelsus identifies cabala with magical astronomy, which is his expression for what we might call operative astrology.[27] In

[25] Thorndike, *A History of Magic and Experimental Science*, V, 130, offers the alternative suggestion that Agrippa's attitude in "De incertitudine" was a pose.
[26] Waite, *The Holy Kabbalah*, p. 456.
[27] Paracelsus, *Opera omnia*, I, 371b, from "De pestilitate, Tractatus I." This treatise is considered spurious by Karl Sudhoff; see his edition of the works of Paracelsus, Munich, 1929–33.

another place cabala is declared to be a part of magic, and earlier writers on medical subjects are censured for not mentioning it.[28] Again, we learn that although once associated with necromancy, cabala is a type of magic, but not necromancy.[29] In yet another place we are informed by this somewhat inconsistent adept that cabalistic magic, in some very unclear way, which does not appear from the text, is concerned with the astral body.[30] Some further elaboration is given to this idea in Paracelsus's work *On the Nature of Things*.[31]

This is not cabalism as it was understood either by the Hebrew cabalists or by their Christian interpreters. Paracelsus was his own cabalist, indeed; it is unfortunate that many occultists, without Waite's knowledge, continue to make the assertion that the cabalistic system is distinctly to be traced in the works of Paracelsus. To some extent it must be admitted that statements like these are themselves passed down from one writer to another with no attempt at inquiry or at verification. Thus it is easy to build up a tremendous list of authorities, references, and testimonials which do not stand up under patient and careful investigation.[32]

There were, however, others to whom cabala was a legitimate part of magic. We know of them largely through the writings of their opponents. For example, Martin del Rio (1551–1608), the Jesuit, writing about 1599, tells us that there are four groups of cabalists. The first and second of these groups, who believe in the fifty gates of understanding and the thirty-two paths of wisdom, respectively, have no connection with magic. The third group, the sephirotists, "begin to smooth the path for superstition." [33]

The large fourth group consists of those who add the twenty-two letters to the fifty gates, thus obtaining seventy-two, which represents both the seventy-two-letter name of God and the seventy-two names of angels, "by the invocation of which miracles are produced

[28] *Ibid.*, I, 405b, from "De peste," I. iii.
[29] *Ibid.*, II, 565b, from "Philosophiae sagacis," Lib. I.
[30] *Ibid.*, II, 56b, from "De vita longa," I. vi.
[31] *Ibid.*, II, 101b, from "De natura rerum liber octavus," chapter, "De separationibus rerum naturalium."
[32] Waite, *The Holy Kabbalah*, pp. 455–56.
[33] Del Rio, *Disquisitionum magicarum libri sex*, p. 54a.

y men, according to Joseph Carnitol, Recanati and others. This is
n entirely blasphemous and magical cabala." [34] The exclusion of
1is group and its work leaves very little to be accepted in the work
f any of the Christian cabalists we have met.

Del Rio's fellow Jesuit, Benedictus Pererius (1535–1610),
1mped cabala with magic, with the interpretation of dreams, and
·ith astrological divination in his book *Against the False and Super-
itious Arts.*[35] The tenth chapter of the first book is devoted to
1balistic magic. Pererius stated that those who asserted cabala to be
science handed down by God to Moses at Mount Sinai were only
certain philosophers of the Jews and some of ours who are more
)ncerned with vanity than with truth and more desirous of learning
1ings curious and unheard of than things true and firm." [36]

The actual description of the cabala which followed this invective
gainst the cabalists was almost to the word a paraphrase of that of
\grippa's *Vanity of the Arts and Sciences.*[37] Pererius then pointed
ut that if there is such a secret knowledge, capable of the perform-
nce of miracles, the miracles recorded in the Scriptures should in-
·olve some mention of the cabala. Finally, and with much justice,
.e remarks that those who are masters of this wisdom ought to use
: to alleviate the condition of their fellow Jews.[38]

In justice to the men of the sixteenth century it should be pointed
ut that there were some who recognized that the association of
abalism and magic was not a product of the true cabala. One such
vas Pierre le Loyer (1550–1634), who understood and illustrated
he valid techniques of cabalistic science, used as a means of develop-
ng the allegorical sense of the Scriptures.[39] The cabalism which is
net in combination with magic is, he maintained, different and the
·roduct of degeneration.[40]

It is not strange that the cabala of the students of magic should
1ave proceeded so far from its original, for it is true that a similar
movement, the practical cabala, went on among the Jewish caba-

4 *Ibid.*, pp. 54a–b.   35 Pererius, *Adversus fallaces et superstitiosas artes.*
6 *Ibid.*, p. 57.   37 *Ibid.*, pp. 57–58; see also Agrippa, *Opera*, II, 68.
8 Pererius, *Adversus fallaces artes*, p. 60.
9 Le Loyer, *Discours, et histoires des spectres*, pp. 892–95.
0 *Ibid.*, pp. 890–91.

lists.[41] But Le Loyer erred in placing specific responsibility for th
degeneration he found. The development of cabala as an adjunct
magic among the Christians came out of Agrippa's reading of Reucl
lin with the deliberate intention of finding there, as Barth said
Agrippa's predecessors, "whatever he wished." [42]

[41] The degenerate form of the cabala among the Jews is the Lurianic cabala pa
ticularly in its practical manifestations. The strictures of Graetz against the enti
movement are largely a product of the excesses of the practical cabalists in Ge
many and, notoriously, in eastern Europe. But see Scholem, *Major Trends*
Jewish Mysticism, for an alternative view.

[42] Thorndike, *History of Magic and Experimental Science*, Vols. V–VI, describ
briefly many other members of the fantastic fringe and their opponents who ma
use of cabalistic materials. This material is incidental to the main theme of Thor
dike's work, however, and his list is, therefore, by no means complete. It is que
tionable whether in one lifetime any scholar could trace all the excesses of the
who cut cabala to suit their interpretations.

VII

THE VERY CHRISTIAN CABALA

THIS STUDY has been restricted, to this point, entirely to published materials. Nothing has been said of the vast amount of manuscript material, spread over the libraries of Europe and America, which would indicate a far greater diffusion of cabalistic knowledge and speculation than can be proved from the printed literature. These manuscripts, in some cases, are extremely early, following closely on the heels of Pico's introduction of the cabala. The greatest concentration of manuscripts, however, comes at that period when publication of cabalistic material fell off, in the middle of the seventeenth century.

A great many of these manuscripts show little originality, and consist of selections from earlier writers, or, at best, commentary on these writers. Some few, however, are documents of merit, worthy to be considered with the major published works of Christian cabalism. In such a survey as this, illustrating the different approaches which make up the Christian interpretation of cabala, the manuscript material cannot be neglected completely.

The verse manuscript which is to be discussed here as representative of its type has been chosen on the basis of its interesting use of cabalistic materials and also because of its historical importance. Pico introduced cabala in Italy very late in the fifteenth century; in the early sixteenth century Ricci and Reuchlin were engaged in cabalistic studies in Germany, Colet and Fisher in England. Pedro Garzia, a Spaniard living in Rome, attacked Pico's cabalistic work as heretical; Erasmus, in Holland, knew enough of the cabala to disapprove of it. The only major European country of the Renaissance which has not been represented in this early period is France. This omission is now to be repaired, by presenting the earliest complete French work of Christian interpretation of cabala.

The author, Jean Thenaud, of Angoulême, was a sixteenth-century Franciscan, of some distinction in the order,[1] who was, according to one author, court poet to Louise de Savoie, the mother of King Francis I.[2] The work we are considering, under the title *The Holy and Very Christian Cabala*, was dedicated to Francis.[3]

Thenaud's Prologue, addressed directly to Francis in laudatory language,[4] begins with an anecdote about Plato, who, it is said, gave thanks to God for three special gifts; first, that he was a reasoning being;[5] second, that he was born an Athenian, in a town where men had true knowledge of God, of the heavens, of the virtues, and of science;[6] and third, that he was born at a time when Socrates could be his teacher.[7] Our author, like Plato, gives thanks for three things in especial. His gratitude, however, is for the complex rather than the simple.

In the first place, he says, he is thankful that, besides being a man, he had been born and reared a Christian and had taken holy orders in Angoulême, where it was his privilege to pray for the king.[8] Secondly, he is grateful for his contact with Louise de Savoie, who assisted him in his studies and in his travels.[9] Because of the kindness of the King's mother, he was able to help in the education of the king.[10] As a return for this kindness, he sends his writings to the king for recreational purposes.[11] Finally, he gives thanks that his previous work found favor in the eyes of the king.[12]

[1] Wadding, *Annales minorum*, V, 118.

[2] D'Orliac, *Francis I, Prince of the Renaissance*, p. 70, where the author is referring to the manuscript which is being discussed here. See Appendix D, "Prologue," lines 39–44. All later references to the text of this manuscript will be given in terms of the line numbers in this appendix of selections.

[3] Thenaud, *La Saincte et trescrestienne cabale*, Dedication.

[4] *Ibid.*, "Prologue," lines 1–4.   [5] *Ibid.*, lines 5–6.   [6] *Ibid.*, lines 7–12.

[7] *Ibid.*, lines 13–16.   [8] *Ibid.*, lines 17–38.

[9] This refers to Thenaud's trip to the Holy Land; see Thenaud, *Le Voyage d'outremer*.

[10] *La Saincte et trescrestienne cabale*, "Prologue," lines 43–54.

[11] *Ibid.*, lines 55–59.

[12] The reference here is to Thenaud, *Triomphe des vertus*, a discussion of which can be found in Paris, *Les Manuscrits françois de la Bibliothèque du Roi*, I, 286–92; IV, 136. The ascription of authorship to Thenaud is made by Paris, *Les Manuscrits françois*, VII, 78–79, in the course of his description of the manuscript of *La Saincte et trescrestienne cabale*, quoting "Prologue," lines 60–77.

Thenaud's intention in this work, he asserts, is to present a brief and accurate account of the "catholic and very holy cabala" in relation to God and the angels, by means of which the king can escape the "frauds and wiles of enemies, visible and invisible" and live in "tranquility, joy, repose, mirth and security," both in this world and in the world to come.[13]

Our author next announces his intention, "as far as the brevity of the treatise permits, to reprove the vicious cabalas, full of errors, and superstitions, of magic, of the Hebrews, and others, equally barbaric, of the Arabs."[14]

When he has prayed the king to accept the work of "a very humble serf and poor peasant,"[15] he gives a chapter by chapter analysis of the contents of the body of the work, beginning

> Your humble serf, by name Thenaud
> The author of this cabalistic poem,
> Divided his poor work, also,
> In tractates three, excluding this, the proem.[16]

The prologue concludes with the author's explanation that the entire book is supposed to be spoken by the spirit of the king's father.[17]

The first book is designed to reveal many wondrous secrets of Paradise in its five chapters.[18] It begins with "the heavenly oracle and cabalistic revelation of the spirit of Monseigneur to the King his son, in his native castle of Cognac."[19] Monseigneur has descended from heaven, he says, to tell his son of the glorious state in which he finds himself.[20] First he tells of the powers of his "fellow citizens of glory," including a comment on the influence of the planets.[21] This comment is picked up again a few pages later, and there Monseigneur advises his son to contemplate the author of their movements.[22] This author, who is in need of no compass or "supermathematical number" to keep the heavenly bodies in their appointed courses is that one God who created souls "clean and pure, immaculate, without spot or blemish, frank, free and virtuous."[23]

---

[13] *Ibid.*, lines 78–100.   [14] *Ibid.*, lines 101–7.   [15] *Ibid.*, lines 108–15.
[16] *Ibid.*, lines 116–18.   [17] *Ibid.*, lines 134–43.   [18] *Ibid.*, lines 119–21.
[19] *Ibid.*, I. i, chapter heading.
[20] *Ibid.*, lines 1–12.   [21] *Ibid.*, lines 13–26.   [22] *Ibid.*, lines 66–91.
[23] *Ibid.*, lines 27–33.

Because he had taken care of his wife, "your superillustrious mother," and of the two children,[24] and because he had ruled with justice and mercy, Monseigneur was well-received in heaven when he died, and soon he found himself among the glorious shades of his ancestors.[25] After he promises his son a description of this region,[26] he begins his actual narrative with "the first and incomprehensible triangle of the divine glory." [27]

This chapter begins with a lengthy glorification of "the eternal and divine nature, in His supreme and immeasurable goodness, who is above the angels," who is "completely indivisible," by whom "all things and every word, affirmative or negative, positive or privative . . . may be heard." [28] This divine nature is triune and is revealed in the triangle of glory.[29] Thus, without being particularly specific about the nature of the three highest of the *sephiroth*, Thenaud has presented them as they were first interpreted by Pico, as symbolic representations of God, manifested as the Father, the Son, and the Holy Spirit.

In this exposition our author says nothing of the names Crown, Wisdom, and Understanding or of the grades of angels assigned by the Hebrew cabalists to these three *sephiroth*. This does not concern him, because he has found a way of rationalizing the Trinity, and this takes precedence in his mind over exactness of exposition. In the later descriptions of the remaining *sephiroth* these names are presented; Thenaud is not omitting them here because of ignorance. His *En Soph*, God, "the eternal and divine nature," in whom all contraries are resolved, who is the very epitome of all the positive qualities, is truly cabalistic, however.

Chapter III is concerned with "the second triangle, called the triangle of triumph, in which are the Seraphim, Cherubim and Thrones, and the sources of Charity, Prudence and Justice." [30] These three angelic orders are, Thenaud says, "the highest and most exalted of created things." [31] Part of their function is to unite the

[24] *Ibid.*, lines 34–37.

[25] *Ibid.*, lines 38–51.

[26] *Ibid.*, lines 52–65.

[27] *Ibid.*, I. ii, chapter heading.

[28] *Ibid.*, lines 1–20.

[29] *Ibid.*, lines 21–36; see also lines 37–48.

[30] *Ibid.*, I. iii, chapter heading.

[31] *Ibid.*, lines 1–4.

love of the Creator and that of the creature.[32] He describes charity, prudence, and justice as "three beautiful rivulets" emanating from seraphim, cherubim, and thrones.[33] This triangle, joined with the first triangle of divine glory, results in a quadrangular figure,[34] which is the source of five different grades of love—divine, angelic, spiritual, animal, and sensual.[35]

This is followed by praise of the seraphim, who are compared with fire,[36] the cherubim, who are lauded for their nearness to the wisdom of God,[37] and the thrones, the heavenly equivalent of the kings and princes on earth.[38] The chapter closes with a paean for those whose fortune it is to reach the exalted realm of the triangle of triumph.[39]

The third triangle, the triangle of victory, constituting the second hierarchy, composed of those ranks of angels, known as powers, principalities, and dominions and representing attributes of force, temperance, and humility, is the subject of Thenaud's fourth chapter.[40] In this chapter the author presents briefly a supernal justification for authority on earth, religious or temporal.[41] Here, too, we find his distinction between angels and souls; angels are completely intellectual and their perfect knowledge is by intuition; souls, on the contrary, are merely rational and syllogizing, gaining understanding of conclusions only from premises.[42] Finally, there are descriptions of the functions of the powers, principalities, and dominions. The section closes with the admission that others have esteemed the place of these three orders higher than has Thenaud, because of the importance of their duties.[43]

The fifth and final chapter of Thenaud's first book is concerned with the classes of heavenly beings called virtues, archangels, and angels, who symbolize the attributes of faith, perseverance, and obedience.[44] Just as the triangles of triumph and glory form the quadrangle of charity, the triangles of victory and combat form the

[32] *Ibid.*, lines 5–7. [33] *Ibid.*, lines 8–15. [34] *Ibid.*, lines 16–25.

[35] *Ibid.*, lines 26–34. [36] *Ibid.*, lines 35–48. [37] *Ibid.*, I. ii, lines 49–52.

[38] *Ibid.*, I. iii, lines 53–62. [39] *Ibid.*, lines 63–72.

[40] *Ibid.*, I. iv, chapter heading. [41] *Ibid.*, lines 1–6.

[42] *Ibid.*, lines 7–19. [43] *Ibid.*, lines 20–27.

[44] *Ibid.*, I. v, chapter heading.

quadrangle of assurance and ease.[45] Thus the entire structure is based upon the "superimperial Trinity." [46] Here Thenaud is carrying a step further the transformation of the *sephiroth* into a bulwark of trinitarianism, which is a characteristic technique of Christian interpretation of the cabala.

It is also worthy of note that the rational soul occupies a medial position; it is of the celestial hierarchy, but is associated with the lowest of the celestial orders. It is not outside, looking in, but inside, looking up.[47] This would seem to be a characteristic locus of rationality among the mystics.

Some further development of this point is to be found in the first two chapters of the second book of Thenaud's exposition, which deal with the doctrine of the worlds and with the place of man in the scheme of things.[48] After a brief introduction, in which Monseigneur begs his son to listen to his words, which are true, not false or frivolous,[49] the angelic, celestial, and elementary worlds are described and distinguished.

The highest of the words, called angelic or intelligible, is filled with the various groups of angelic beings, all adoring the triune monarchy.[50] Next, there is the celestial or mobile world, forever turning about the Arctic and Antarctic poles, divided into nine heavens, in which are the planetary influences, heavenly bodies, and clear stars.[51] Finally there is the elementary world, composed of nine circles, which is "variable, unstable, material, corruptible, and mobile" and is dependent upon the other two worlds.[52]

As fire is the heating principle in the elementary world, the sun is the vivifying principle in the celestial world and the seraphim the beatifying principle in the angelic world.[53] Water, in the elementary world, parallels the moon in the celestial world and the cherubic wisdom in the angelic world.[54] In fact, there is nothing in the world we perceive which has not its exemplar in the superior worlds.[55]

The pattern of the worlds to this point is deterministic. While it

[45] *Ibid.*, lines 1–6.   [46] *Ibid.*, lines 7–13.   [47] *Ibid.*, lines 14–30.
[48] *Ibid.*, "Prologue," lines 122–23.   [49] *Ibid.*, II. i, lines 1–5.
[50] *Ibid.*, lines 6–19.   [51] *Ibid.*, lines 20–31.   [52] *Ibid.*, lines 32–61.
[53] *Ibid.*, lines 62–73.   [54] *Ibid.*, lines 74–79.   [55] *Ibid.*, lines 80–85.

is not identical with the pattern set up by the cabalistic doctrine of worlds, it is sufficiently similar to have been accepted into the Christian interpretation of the cabala from the time of Pico. This doctrine shares with the Hebrew doctrine the notion of the exemplary character of the higher levels and the resultant determinism. Into this pattern we must now fit free will for men.

Cabalists introduce free will by means of the concepts of the thirty-two paths of wisdom and the fifty gates of understanding, through mastery of which man is enabled to progress from sphere to sphere and from world to world. Thenaud gains the same end by making a fourth world of man, the "miraculous microcosm who has neither form nor place to himself but can make himself whatever he wishes to be." [56] No other creature is capable of this.[57] Man is, however, because the three parts of his body form an image of the three other worlds.[58] This is an echo of the cabalistic doctrine of *Adam kadmon*.

The remainder of the second chapter of Thenaud's second book elaborates on the possibilities of man's self-determination and concludes with an exhortation to holy love and to purgation by means of the sacraments and of contemplation.[59]

In his third chapter Thenaud condemns as superstitious the use of cabala by believers in magic for purposes of "arithmancy" and "theomancy." He disapproves particularly of the attribution of "superstitions, curious writings, and vain fictions," not only in philosophy but even in theology, to great men of past ages [60] and of the consideration of Moses as "prince of magic." [61] Among the books which he censures are the Hebrew *Raziel* and the works of Hermes Trismegistus. He asks very pointedly why, if it be true that the Hebrews have mastery of this magical technique, they have not used it to better their own situation.[62] A man who leads a holy life, not one who believes in magic, is worthy of the revelation of the cabala.[63]

In the fourth and final chapter of this second book Thenaud ex-

---

[56] *Ibid.*, II. ii, lines 1–4.   [57] *Ibid.*, lines 4–22.   [58] *Ibid.*, lines 23–27.
[59] *Ibid.*, lines 28–37.   [60] *Ibid.*, II. iii, lines 1–12.   [61] *Ibid.*, line 13.
[62] *Ibid.*, lines 14–37. This argument was used by others besides Thenaud; see Pererius, *Adversus fallaces artes*, p. 60.
[63] *La Saincte et trescrestienne cabale*, II. iii, lines 38–44.

pands this statement and tells what is the true and holy cabala and who are the cabalists. The true cabalists are the Christians who follow the Evangelists and the Gospels and perform the obligations of their faith.[64]

The third book of the *Very Christian Cabala* is devoted to the exposition of Thenaud's number system and to the details of the way in which the higher worlds influence and govern the lower. Thus, unity is the number properly applied to God alone; it is infinite and incomprehensible. Application of the concept of unity to God does not affect the profound mystery of the Trinity, for unity does not destroy trinity.[65] Ten, the number of the Tetractys, represents the angelic world.[66] The angels and the archangels are hierarchically represented by the numbers to ten; parenthetically, the fact that the names of these angelic beings end in either *yah* or *el* is explained in terms of the dual character of God as just and merciful, a common cabalistic belief.[67] The third number, or, rather, type of number, is the mixed, or composite. This represents the confusion and instability of the world of things and is the number by means of which the celestial world influences the world of elements.[68] Thus the pattern of government and rule is represented by numbers, a device common to all numerological speculations, rather than specifically cabalistic.

The remainder of Thenaud's third book is devoted to amplification of the "mixed" numbers and to a discussion of the parallel between God, as the source of the entire structure of being, and the sun, as the secondary source of one section of that structure. In his conclusion Thenaud exhorts the king to humility and a religious life and, incidentally, dates his work in the twenty-fifth year of Francis's life, or 1519.[69]

Since this was not Thenaud's only book on the cabala,[70] although

[64] *Ibid.*, II. iv, lines 1–16.   [65] *Ibid.*, III. i, lines 1–12.
[66] *Ibid.*, lines 13–26.   [67] *Ibid.*, lines 27–34.   [68] *Ibid.*, lines 35–54.
[69] *Ibid.*, "Epilogue," lines 1–4. Francis I was born September 12, 1494.
[70] Thorndike, *History of Magic and Experimental Science*, VI, 452–53, discusses briefly a manuscript of a different treatise on the cabala written by Thenaud in 1536, apparently at the request of Francis I. This manuscript is at the University of Geneva (MS Français, No. 167); see Senebier, *Catalogue raisonné des manuscrits de Genève*, p. 420. Another manuscript of 205 leaves, described as "L'Introduction

it seems to have been his earliest, it is not surprising that his knowledge of the subject seems so full. His poem gives a partial and somewhat distorted picture of cabala, because he presents no information about the exegetical techniques of the cabalists. His discussion of the doctrine of the worlds is full, as is his presentation of the *sephiroth*. In his section dealing with numbers, there is more than a suggestion that he was familiar with Reuchlin's work on the cabala, just as in other sections the influence of Pico is felt.

Although Thenaud's work is apparently the earliest complete work on the cabala written in France, it is not the first in which reference to cabala is made. It has already been pointed out [71] that Lazarelli and Jacques le Fevre d'Etaples knew of the cabala at about the time that Pico first wrote about it. Of the same circle of humanists was Symphorien Champier (1472–1539), who published some unimportant comments on the cabala in the second book of his *Pronosticon*, which was concerned with the prophecies of astrologers.[72]

Among the writers who came later than Thenaud, one especially deserving of mention is Guillaume Postel (1510–1581), a mildly abnormal erudite, whom, for no particularly clear reason, such occult historians of the occult tradition as Eliphas Levi have picked as one of the mahatmas of the Western world.[73] Postel's major contribution to the Christian interpretation of the cabala was his Latin translation of the *Book of Formation*.[74] Had the translation of the Zohar on which he worked been published, he might have merited even more consideration.[75]

Postel did, however, make casual use of cabalistic materials in several of his books. In his *History . . . of the Tartars, Persians,*

---

en la cabale," dedicated in verse to Francis I (MSS de la Bibl. de Nantes, No. 521) may be a copy of either the Paris manuscript which I have used or the later Geneva manuscript used by Thorndike. Gautier-Vignal, *Pic de la Mirandole*, quotes from but does not identify a manuscript by Thenaud in which there was a direct ascription to Pico.

[71] See above, chap. ii.   [72] Champier, *Pronosticon*.

[73] See Levi, *Histoire de la magie*, pp. 347–48.

[74] Postel, *Abrahami patriarchae liber Jezirah*.

[75] This manuscript, long hunted and by many writers suspected of being mythical, was discovered by Perles in the Munich Staatsbibliothek as Cod. Lat. 7428 (Genesis). Perles's discovery has been verified by Scholem.

Arabs, Turks and All the Other Ishmaelites he refers to the Zohar and to the secret doctrine of the Hebrews.[76] In his *De orbis terrae concordia* he talks of the proof of the Trinity by cabalistic means.[77]

Pontus de Tyard (1521–1605), one of the group of writers making up the Pleiad, wrote also on philosophical and scientific subjects. In a dialogue which had the merit of presenting the Copernican system, but also the demerit of remaining noncommittal about its value, Tyard has one of his characters, who advances the religious arguments against the heliocentric world view, include references to both Talmudists and cabalists.[78]

Philip de Mornay (1549–1623) included many cabalistic references and a chapter on the cabala according to Pico della Mirandola in a work on the truth of Christianity.[79] Jean Belot (fl. 1570) cited cabalistic authors in opposing the occult system of Agrippa [80] and added other references in describing various systems of divination.[81]

It is not, however, with any sense that these other French writers who touched on the cabala are indebted to Thenaud for their interest in the subject that Thenaud's work has been treated in so much detail here. He has been so presented for two reasons. In the first place, in his work the cabala was used as a peg on which to hang moral instruction. In this respect he is unlike the authors previously presented. In the second place, Thenaud's work is here a surrogate for all the manuscript writings of Christian interpretation of the cabala.

Before any definite historical treatment of the Christian interpreters can be given, all these manuscripts which are preserved should be analyzed for originality of source and originality of thought. For this study of types of Christian interpretation *The Holy and Very Christian Cabala*, because of its early date, because of its association with the court of the king of France, and because of the distinction of its author in the Franciscan movement, is a sufficient exemplar.

[76] Postel, *Histoire . . . des Tartares, Persiens, Arabes, Turcs*, II, 21, 26.
[77] Postel, *De orbis terrae concordia*, pp. 23, 259.   [78] De Tyard, *L'Univers*.
[79] De Mornay, *The Trewnesse of the Christian Religion*, pp. 533 ff.; see also pp. 71–73, 437, 474, 483, and the unpaged "Preface to the Reader."
[80] Belot, *Les Fleurs de la philosophie chrestienne et morale*.
[81] Belot, *Instruction . . . pour apprendre les sciences de chiromancie et phisiognomie*.

VIII

THE ERUDITES

THUS FAR, the major emphasis of this study of the diffusion of cabalistic ideas in Renaissance Europe has been on those outstanding individuals in the Christian cabalistic tradition who, by their studies, created the Christian interpretation of the cabala. Important names have been paraded in an attempt to show the introduction of the particular concepts which Christianized the cabala. Essentially, to this point, this has been a discussion of the pioneers of Christian interpretation of cabala. Only a few representatives of their followers have been noticed, to show the immediate spread of these ideas.

It remains to be demonstrated that, if not a popular movement, at least the diffusion of cabalistic knowledge rested upon too broad a base for it to be considered the pastime of a limited few esoterics. Too much has been made by our present-day crop of theosophists of the isolated character of those Christian cabalists who have been discussed here. They have been too often considered as isolated peak figures, as mahatmas of occidental culture.[1] It is in belated justice that it is here pointed out that the Christian cabalists of the Renaissance were men of their own times, following in all fields of endeavor the cultural pattern of their times, not Indianized Europeans of the twentieth century.

Few of the students who are to be discussed here took cabalism seriously as a philosophy. It had rapidly proved a blind alley for Christian thought. Pico and Reuchlin were trying to use cabala as

[1] See, *inter alia*, the treatment of Pico, Reuchlin, and Agrippa in Waite, *The Holy Kabbalah*; Levi, *Transcendental Magic*; Westcott, *Introduction to the Kabalah*; see also the scattered references in Madame Blavatsky's formidable *Isis Unveiled*. But note that Thorndike, *A History of Magic and Experimental Science*, V, 233, says, "Several allusions to the cabala and cabalists have suggested its presence in the thought of the time."

the basis for an eclectic system which would harmonize the philosophies of classical antiquity with Christian thought. They believed
they had found an instrument to suit their need. They did not realize, as we, from the vantage point of the present, can realize, which
were the vital forms of thought in their day. They selected, rather,
a path which has become less and less important as the years have
passed.

With a few minor exceptions, therefore, such as Robert Fludd
(1574–1637) who like Paracelsus was his own cabalist, and the
Cambridge Platonists, the successors to the Christian cabalists who
have been presented in the previous sections of this book are not to
be found among the philosophers, but among the erudites. Philologians and grammarians will be found to have used the cabalistic
techniques as a tool in their work. Historians, writing of the Jewish
past, will accept the Christian cabala as valid source material. Minor
theologians and commentators on the Scriptures used the cabala as
authority to bolster up a doubtful point of interpretation. In the end
we shall see that some knowledge of cabala was part of the equip-
ment of every scholar in every part of Europe.

The first group of erudites to be presented here are those who in
later centuries might have been called historians of culture. The first
of these is Louis Ricchieri (c.1450–1525), who published, as early
as 1517, a volume called *Lectionum antiquarum*.[2] Ricchieri's information about the cabala came from Pico.[3] He asserts that there
are three types of Hebrew thought: Talmudic, which is heretical;
philosophical, which is late, coming after the time of Averroës; and
cabalistic, which is "the oldest of all, and true more than any other:
because established opinion is that it was made known to Moses by
God, the greatest and best." [4] This is followed by the standard description of the handing down of the tradition to the seventy elders,
and so forth.[5] The most surprising fact about this treatment is that
it should exist at all. Of course, Reuchlin, Ricci, and others had also
written about cabala by the time that Ricchieri used Pico as his

---

[2] Ricchieri, *Lectionum antiquarum*, first printed at Basle, 1517; I have used the
edition published at Geneva, 1620.
[3] *Ibid.*, p. 493.   [4] *Ibid.*   [5] *Ibid.*, pp. 493–94.

source. It is still amazing that cabala should make its way into the works of the learned within twenty-five years of its introduction into Europe.

Sixty years later "established opinion" was less firmly established. Francis Vallesius, writing about the treatment of physics in the Scriptures,[6] in 1587, follows the argument of Agrippa's *Vanity of the Arts and Sciences*. He considers the cabalists as a species of Hebrew magi, and charges that the cabalistic claim to the performance of miracles by means of words is a form of incantation.

The magi, of whom Zoroaster, King of the Bactrians, is thought to have been the chief, followed this opinion . . . and, among the Hebrews, those called cabalists, who boast their doctrine to have been derived from more secret revelations of God, promise that they will produce some sort of miracles by words and characters. Moreover the opinion held at all times concerning incantations seems even to awake confidence in them.[7]

The criticism which Vallesius offers of this type of belief in the power of words, whether its source be in cabalism or any other similar movement, is related to conceptualism. Words have no power in themselves, only a meaning assigned to them by man.

Even though the vain and superstitious magi and cabalists and those who consider themselves the most inspired, the Platonists, heap up so many things, it is truly false and foreign to all reason for any power to reside in words themselves, or anything else except what they mean according to the acceptance of men.[8]

One year later, in 1588, Thomas Garzonus (1549–1589) compiled an encyclopedia of belief [9] in which a complete discourse is devoted to the cabala.[10] Although the author mentions Ricci,[11] he uses Reuchlin as his major source and Pico as his minor. He distinguishes between a true and false cabala by claiming ancient origin of the true cabala. The division of the true cabala into *Breshit*, or cosmology, and *Mercava*, or symbolic theology, is drawn directly

[6] Vallesius, *De iis, quae scripta sunt physice in libris sacris*, Book I.
[7] *Ibid.*, p. 66.   [8] *Ibid.*, p. 68.
[9] Thomas Garzonus, *La Piazza universale*.
[10] *Ibid.*, Disc. xxix, "De Cabalisti," pp. 247–68.   [11] *Ibid.*, p. 248.

from Reuchlin, as is the list of cabalistic authors which is quoted. Here we meet once more, as in the *Apology* of Archangelus and Reuchlin's *De arte cabalistica,* the same words in praise of Joseph Gikatilia: "But in the judgment of many, no one has written of this science more skillfully, more distinctly, more clearly, than Rabbi Joseph ben Abraham Castiliensis, citizen of Salerno, in his book entitled *A Garden of Nuts.*" [12] Garzonus is an encyclopedist pure and simple; he tells what is known, but fails to criticize in any respect.

One of the earliest references to the cabala in a history of philosophy is found in a work published in 1655.[13] This reference in George Horn's work is interesting in that it is an early notice of the similarity between the cabala and the late Greek mystery cults.[14] This is much the same as the more scholarly and more critical ascription of Gnostic parallels and sources to cabalistic ideas which is found in the work of Franck.[15]

Once more in the erudite work of the Jesuit Menochio (1576–1655),[16] the distinction is made between a good and a bad cabala.[17] The good cabala is concerned with philosophic generalizations, like those of Pico; the second type, or bad cabala, is concerned with the manipulations of words and their letters and is Pythagorean in character.[18] Interestingly, with the exception of the quotation from Pico all Menochio's sources are secondary.

Another Jesuit, Caspar Knittel (fl. 1680), fittingly closes this group of historians of culture, because his work, like Pico's, is an attempt at synthesis of cultures.[19] The fourth part of this work deals with cabala and Pythagoreanism, under the title "The Universal Art of the Hebrews and Pythagoreans for knowing (or rather being ignorant)." [20] Knittel asserts that cabala consists entirely in the manipulation of the alphabet and the use of the letters as numbers.

---

[12] *Ibid.*, p. 252.   [13] George Horn, *Historiae philosophicae.*
[14] *Ibid.*, p. 38.   [15] Franck, *Kabbalah*, p. 101; see also pp. 220–38.
[16] Menochio, *Le stuore, overo trattenimenti eruditi*, Parte Prima.
[17] *Ibid.*, p. 22.
[18] *Ibid.*, p. 21, where one of Pico's conclusions is cited as an example of the "good" cabala.
[19] Knittel, *Via regia ad omnes scientias et artes.*   [20] *Ibid.*, p. 99.

He follows the distinction between *bereshith* and *merkavah*, and gives the schema of the ten *sephiroth* together with a discussion of the influence of the names of God in the lower world.[21] This description is accredited to Pico (though Pico nowhere schematized the *sephiroth*), and its tone is one of opposition to cabala. It is followed by a discussion of the Pythagorean "cabala," or number symbolism.

The next group of erudites to be considered here took magic in its various forms as their subject. This does not imply that they practiced magic or believed in it. Some of them did; others were opposed to magic; a third division maintained an attitude of reserved judgment, studying magic without bias. So, for example, Anania, writing in 1589 on the nature of demons,[22] said that the demons are of equal standing with the angels and that the cabalists err in believing them subordinate to the angels.[23] Later he defined cabala as a form of magical superstition worked out in terms of letters and numbers.[24] We can see from the tone of this definition that its author was not a believer in magic; at the same time, his earlier censure of the cabalists for their unfairness to the demons makes clear that he was not an opponent of magic. He merely tried to give the devil his due.

Caspar Peucer (1525-1602), in 1593, wrote a commentary on the principal types of divination.[25] Although he was by no means favorable to the cabala, some aspects displeased him less than others. The strength of his opposition is indicated in this passage:

There is no lie more offensive, greater and more insulting to God than to imagine that by the recital of the name or word of God the means which are being used assume immediately a new force able to effect either things most severely prohibited by God, like murders, thefts, injuries of various kinds and other things of this sort, or works which God alone effects by his omnipotence: such is the falsehood of the cabalists who claim that they perform those things which they promise so magnificently and which they accomplish sometimes with the help of the devil and the permission of God, by means of the ten names of the true God and of the angels, which the Scriptures mention.[26]

[21] *Ibid.*, pp. 99-118.   [22] Anania, *De natura daemonum.*
[23] *Ibid.*, p. 9.   [24] *Ibid.*, p. 88.
[25] Peucer, *Commentarius de praecipuis divinationum generibus.*   [26] *Ibid.*, p. 323.

This is certainly vigorous opposition. It rests upon a basis of information derived from Pico and Reuchlin, as may be seen from the author's discussion of the twofold cabala [27] and his lengthy definition derived from the etymology of the name "cabala":

There are those who derive [the word "Sibyl"] from Hebrew, and assert that it arose, with some change of letters, from the word "Kabala," which, formed from the verb "Kibel," means a doctrine not implanted in souls by nature, or transferred with the seed by parents, nor noticed by practice or experience, nor brought forth and forced out from nature, nor drawn out of books composed by human wisdom: but promulgated by Divine Providence, and, as it were, infused into the souls of the holy prophets by God Himself and proved and approved by the voice and heavenly testimonies. For the word "Kibel" means received, accepted, hence "Kabala," that is, a doctrine accepted from heavenly admission or disclosure. [28]

This is, perhaps, in our opinion, an insufficient basis for hostile judgment; in the sixteenth century, it was enough. But Peucer moderated his antipathy in one instance, where cabalistic techniques were used to prove fundamental doctrines of his Church.

Much more pleasing is the contrivance of those who deduce the time of birth, crucifixion, resurrection and triumph of our Saviour, Jesus Christ, from the letters of the Hebrew title of the first book of Moses. This book is called Brescith, which they derive from the root Barscith, that is, I shall give a son. The time of the giving of the Son, that is, of the coming of the Messiah, they determine [by various numerological methods]. . . . If these numbers are added, they amount to four thousand years. Moreover, Christ was taken up into heaven and placed on the right hand of the Eternal Father, conqueror of the Devil, death and hell, in the year 3996 after the beginning of the world, a number which lacks four years of the complete four millennia. [29]

Such speculations please our author more than the practical or wonder-working aspects of Christian cabala. He recommends that

[27] Ibid., p. 411.   [28] Ibid., p. 263.
[29] Ibid., p. 417. I have omitted the details of the arithmetical process by which four thousand is achieved.

anyone who engages his wits in such matters should not be censured.[30]

A decade later Cesare della Riviera published his erudite tome on the magic world of heroes.[31] He discusses the ascription of numerical structure to the world by various groups and includes the cabalists who use the *sephiroth* "to describe God, the Divine Providence, and the universe of things." [32] Unique among these erudites is Della Riviera; of all of them he alone has learned from Reuchlin the doctrine of *Adam kadmon*, or the primordial man, the doctrine which equates the *sephiroth* to the parts of a human body. This doctrine he presents, together with the alternative theory that the *sephiroth* represent a tree, whose roots are the three highest *sephiroth*, whose trunk is *tifereth*, and whose branches are the other six *sephiroth*. The same passage contains a glorification of the sun.[33]

The author discusses various trinities in Orphism, Zoroastrianism, cabalism, and Christianity.[34] The seed of Pico was still sprouting. Some twenty pages are given to expanding Latin words into phrases to be used in magic and alchemy; the expansion accords with Della Riviera's understanding of the technique of notarikon. Thus, "caelum" is expanded into "caelestium lumen," [35] "quinta essentia" into "quintum tale, est Secretum semen naturae terra iacens," [36] "Diana" into "diem afferens naturae," [37] and many others. Astrology also appears to be one of the aspects of the cabala, for Della Riviera's last comment on the cabalists is that they believe that even the plants grow through sidereal influence.[38]

Cigogna, shortly after this, referred to cabala as the oldest of the sciences.[39] He states correctly that "in the Hebrew language, they call this occult science cabala which means reception, because this science was never written down, but was learned by one from another by word of mouth and was handed down as if from hand to hand." [40] He tells of the doctrine of infinite worlds and recites the Scriptural testimonies to support this doctrine; [41] of all the erudites,

[30] *Ibid.*, p. 417.

[31] Della Riviera, *Il magico mondo de gli heroi.*

[32] *Ibid.*, p. 28.

[33] *Ibid.*, pp. 31–32.   [34] *Ibid.*, pp. 45–46.

[35] *Ibid.*, pp. 49–50.   [36] *Ibid.*, pp. 51–52.   [37] *Ibid.*, p. 53.

[38] *Ibid.*, p. 121.   [39] D. Strozzius Cigogna, *Magiae omnifariae*, p. 129.

[40] *Ibid.*   [41] *Ibid.*, pp. 130–33.

he is the only writer to treat this aspect of cabalistic speculation.

Next we find cabala tied up with alchemy, in a collection of Paracelsan formulas for the transmutation of metals by Gerardus Dorneus.[42] Dorneus expressed a very high opinion of the cabala. "The cabala itself seems to build a road for men to God by anagogy . . . for cabala is full of divine mysteries." [43]

Jacques Gaffarel (1601–1681), who analyzed manuscripts of Recanati and others which, he maintains, were used by Pico,[44] reveals some slight part of his knowledge of cabala in a book called *Curiositez inouyes*.[45] He refers to the interpretation of dreams by Daniel, saying:

And just as it was fit for Daniel only, who was just before the Lord, to interpret it, the Hebrews say likewise that it is fit only for good people and not for all sorts of people to interpret that which one sees in heaven, which is most often obscure and difficult, and that GEMATRIE, NO-TARICON and TEMURAH, which are the three divisions of the cabala are very necessary to know in order to interpret it perfectly.[46]

Gaffarel shows familiarity with Reuchlin, Pico, and Agrippa and cites "the ten names called by the Hebrews, ZEPHIROTZ." [47]

Writing of the secret salt of philosophers,[48] De Nuysement referred to the existence of seventy cabalistic books and quoted Pico on this subject. After mentioning how reverently Pico spoke of these books [49] and quoting from Pico's *Apologia*, he went on to say: "Moreover they are held in such veneration that no Hebrew under the age of forty is allowed to touch them. And this is to be marveled at, that in this cabalistic doctrine some major teachings of Christianity are contained." [50]

A final comment in this division of our subject can be cited from the Jesuit Menestrier (1631–1705), who wrote, in 1689, about the philosophy of enigmatic images.[51] Writing "Of the Enigmas of the Cabala," this author says:

[42] Dorneus, *Congeries Paracelsicae chemiae de transmutationum metallorum.* This is included in Zetznerus, ed., *Theatrum chemicum,* I, 533–619.
[43] *Ibid.*, p. 595.   [44] Gaffarel, *Codicum cabbalisticorum manuscriptorum.*
[45] Gaffarel, *Curiositez inouyes, passim.*   [46] *Ibid.*, p. 306.
[47] *Ibid.*, p. 201.   [48] De Nuysement, *Tractatus de vero sale secreto philosophorum.*
[49] *Ibid.*, p. 188.   [50] *Ibid.*, p. 189.
[51] Menestrier, *La Philosophie des images enigmatiques.*

There are two kinds of cabala. One is that of the Jews, which is based only on the mysteries of the Scriptures, or, more, on the reveries of the Rabbis, and the other is that of the alchemists who seek the Philosopher's Stone. The one is no less extravagant than the other, save that the former are concerned with theological matters, and the latter with physics.[52]

A considerable group of erudites were descendants of Reuchlin, the Hebraist, rather than Reuchlin, the cabalist. From the time of Reuchlin the study of the Hebrew language became more common among the Christians of Europe than it had been. Because this study, in its turn, led to closer application to the Hebrew text of the Old Testament and to critical comment thereon, Reuchlin has been considered one of the precursors of the Protestant movement. Among the philologians, grammàrians, and exegetes of the century and a half after Reuchin, many used cabalistic material in their published works. It is to this group that we turn now for examples of the diffusion of knowledge about the cabala.

Priority in this group, by virtue of his name, goes to Anton Reuchlin, who composed his primer of Hebrew about the middle of the sixteenth century.[53] In the course of his explanations of the words in six of the Psalms, our author has occasion to interpret the Tetragrammaton. This he does by referring to John Reuchlin and to Galatinus, and he adapts their explanation in this way:

By the letter Iod is understood the Father, who is the origin and source of all things. By the letter He, the Son, through whom all things which are made began to be. By Vav, which is conjunctive and copulative, is understood the Holy Ghost who is the love and bond of both.[54]

Fabricius, forty years later, in a discussion of *Schem Hamphorasch,* makes the same point about the Tetragrammaton as a symbol of Trinity.[55] This writer, after developing Reuchlin's explanation of the seventy-two letter name of God from Exodus xiv. 19–21, makes what is perhaps one of the foulest comments ever to be published in a theological work.

[52] *Ibid.,* p. 281.
[53] Anton Reuchlin, *Tabulae viginti, institutiones in linguam sanctam.*
[54] *Ibid.,* "Exegesis," p. 8.
[55] Fabricius, *De Schem Hamphorasch usu, et abusu apud Iudaeos,* pp. D2r–v.

First that sacred Schemhamphoras has degenerated; it is no longer the name of God explained by the Holy Trinity; it is not a symbol of hidden mystery and more secret knowledge, in which only the devout rejoiced, before the incarnation of Christ. Now Schemhamphorasch has become Scham happeresch—there is the dung.[56]

Next we come to the disputed question of the antiquity of Hebrew vowel points. Hebrew is always written, and usually printed, without vowels. In order to preserve the exact text of the Scriptures in an age which was forgetting Hebrew, the Massoretes developed a method of indicating the vocalization of Hebrew by means of points imposed on the consonants as superscripts or subscripts. The earlier Christian Hebraists, knowing nothing of this history, could not decide whether or not this system of vocalization was ancient or modern, whether, in fact, the vocalization of the Scriptures had not been fixed at Sinai.

One of the early contributors to this controversy was Ludovicus Cappellus (1585–1658), who, in 1624, wrote about the mysteries of Hebrew vowels.[57] Cappellus believed that the vowel points and accents of the Hebrew text were of comparatively recent invention, and the argument he used was based on the practices of the cabalists.

There are also other cabalistic writers (besides those ancient ones) who have applied themselves in every age to digging out different allegories and mysteries from the Scripture. Now, truly, all of these, whether early and ancient or more recent, strive to elicit and amass their mystic foolishness, and beautiful allegories, or, rather, their monstrous comments from the consonants or letters of the Hebrew text alone, by inverting them, by metathesis, or by various multiplex permutation, either by notarikon or by what they call gematria or by *atbash* or by some other cabalistic method of permutation of letters. Altogether, they dig none of their allegories or mystic interpretations out of the vowel points or accents; quite the reverse, among them there is silence concerning these.[58]

The younger Buxtorf (1599–1664) answered Cappellus in his treatise concerning the punctuation, vowels, and accents in the He-

[56] *Ibid.*, pp. E8v–F1r.   [57] Cappellus, *Arcanum punctationis revelatum.*
[58] *Ibid.*, pp. 25–26.

brew Old Testament.[59] Where Cappellus, in order to make his
point, had asserted that the Zohar and *Sefer ha-Bahir* were late
pseudepigrapha,[60] Buxtorf gathers up testimony to the antiquity of
these primary cabalistic texts from a variety of Hebrew sources.[61]
The number of these citations evidences Buxtorf's superior mastery
of the Hebrew language. Since these texts are established by authority as very ancient, their statement that vocalization is a part of the
Oral Law is to be accepted.

Johannes Leusden (1624–1699) reviewed the controversy in his
philological tracts,[62] but adds nothing to the discussion; he is in-
clined to agree with Buxtorf that Hebrew vowel points are of great
antiquity. There is no advance in knowledge shown in his work or in
that of Uythage, who went through the materials some years
later.[63]

Leusden is also the author of a discourse "De Kabbala et Kab-
balistis," which is included in his *Philologus Hebraeus*.[64] This discourse is almost entirely based upon Menasseh ben Israel's *Con-
ciliator*, and it repeats Menasseh's citations from Hebrew cabalistic
literature. In addition, Leusden quotes Pico and Reuchlin's *De arte
cabalistica*. His chief conclusion is that the cabala is of great age.

Other philologians and exegetes who refer to the cabala in the
course of their writings include Leonard Marius,[65] Thomas Godwyn,[66] André Rivet,[67] Nicholas Abramus,[68] Peter Cunaeus,[69] Al-

---

[59] Buxtorf, the Younger, *Tractatus de punctorum, vocalium et accentuum.*
[60] Cappellus, *Arcanum punctationis,* pp. 192–97.
[61] Buxtorf, *Tractatus de punctorum,* pp. 68–75.
[62] Leusden, *Philologus Hebraeus,* first published in 1657; I have used the 3d ed.,
Utrecht, 1686, pp. 143–94.
[63] Uythage, *Revelatio punctationis dissertatio.*
[64] Leusden, *Philologus Hebraeus,* pp. 309–25.
[65] Marius, *Commentariorum in universam Sanctam Scripturam,* "Digressio de Nominibus Dei," pp. 420–35.
[66] Godwyn, *Moses and Aaron;* this was a very popular work; it went through
many editions, of which the first was published in London, 1624. The 1667 edition,
which I used, was the ninth.
[67] Rivet, *Exercitationes cxc in Genesim,* especially pp. 210–11.
[68] Abramus, *Pharus veteris testamenti:* "De Cabbala Hebraeorum" (VII. ii);
"Noteriacon nominis Abram" (VII, iii).
[69] Cunaeus, *De republica Hebraeorum,* especially pp. 240–42.

lard Uchtmann,[70] August Pfeiffer,[71] John Spencer,[72] Johannes Benedict Carpzov,[73] Jacob Alting,[74] Campegius Vitringa,[75] and Andreas Sennert.[76]

To show how the theologians used cabalistic materials for their ends, we may consider the controversial work of Peter Allix (1641–1717) against the Unitarians.[77] Probably the only Jewish sources which can be twisted into a defense of Trinitarian ideas are cabalistic; this can be done only by close study of the Christian interpreters of the cabala.

Although Allix has little respect for the cabalists, he uses their arguments as far as he can. He speaks of the work of the cabalists as ridiculous and useless.

I know very well that the method of those cabalistical men, who seek for mysteries almost in every letter of the words of Scripture, hath made them justly ridiculous. And indeed one cannot imagine an occupation more vain or useless, than the prodigious labour which they undergo in their way of gematria, notarikon, and tsirouph.[78]

His knowledge of Hebrew does not seem to be very extensive. Most of his quotations of the Hebrew sources come by way of Latin translations incorporated in the words of other writers. He does, however, seem to be thoroughly familiar with the work of Menahem Recanati, who is quoted no less than thirty times in the book. The only other writer who is quoted almost as frequently is Reuchlin, whose *De*

---

[70] Uchtmann, tr., *Bechinat ha-olam*, by Jedaiah Penini ben Abraham Bedarsi, especially pp. 314–20. Uchtmann was Professor of Hebrew at Leyden.

[71] Pfeiffer, *Opera omnia*, includes his *Critica sacra*, of which chap. vii, "De Kabbala," pp. 746–50, denies the contributions of cabala to Christianity.

[72] Spencer, *De legibus Hebraeorum ritualibus*, especially I, 164. The author was dean of Ely Cathedral and prefect of Corpus Christi College, Cambridge.

[73] Carpzov, *Introductio in theologiam Judaicam*, prefaced to Martin, *Pugio fidei*; see especially chaps. v and vi; see also, Carpzov, *Apparatus historico-criticus*, especially pp. 532–37.

[74] Alting, *Opera*, V, heptade 5, "Dissertatio de cabbala scripturaria."

[75] Vitringa, *Sacrarum observationum*, I, 114–40.

[76] Sennert, *Exercitationum philologicarum*, dissertation iii, "De Cabbalah."

[77] Allix, *The Judgment of the Ancient Jewish Church against the Unitarians.*

[78] *Ibid.*, p. 127.

arte cabalistica is canvassed for every possible Trinitarian suggestion.[79]

Johannes Hoornbeeck (1617–1666), whose major object in life was missionary activity among the Jews and any other non-Christian folk he could find, in his *Summa* of religious controversies [80] answers in the negative the question:

Whether the cabalistic doctrine, which consists chiefly in the permutation of letters, by themurah, as they call it; or in arithmetical computation of them, by gematria; or in the formation of various words from one, by notarikon; besides the other modes or rules, of which the Jews have thirteen in all . . . whether this doctrine is divine or certain.[81]

Apparently Hoornbeeck did not feel that the results obtained by Reuchlin in developing Christian doctrine out of the Old Testament were of sufficient value to justify the acceptance of these techniques.

This author has a more extended discussion in his long work on convincing and converting the Jews.[82] Here he refers to the cabala as bipartite, consisting of the Oral Law and "that special part of it, which consists in a sort of mystical logic, by means of which they draw out secret senses of the Law in a marvelous manner." [83] Later he says of cabala, "it contains more of folly than of truth," [84] and suggests that anything mentioned in cabala should be checked with the Scriptures to see whether it is deserving of acceptance. It is most unbecoming to compare this doctrine with Holy Writ, he says, because it is fitter for sport than for serious study. Finally, he sums up his views on the cabalists in the blunt statement, "With great effort, they produce great follies." [85]

Many more names might be mentioned here. There would, however, be little point in multiplying examples. Enough has been shown to prove that knowledge of the cabala was not a phenomenon limited to a few, but that its spread was wide. It was not the sacro-

---

[79] Most of the cabalistic material is quoted on pp. 127–46.

[80] Hoornbeeck, *Summa controversiarum religionis.*   [81] *Ibid.,* pp. 72–73.

[82] Hoornbeeck, *Teshubat yehudah; sive, Pro convincendis et convertendis Judaeis,* pp. 89–95, "Num kabalistica Judaeorum doctrina divinae sit originis et authoritatis?"

[83] *Ibid.,* p. 89.   [84] *Ibid.,* p. 94.   [85] *Ibid.,* p. 95.

sanct possession of any one class of erudites. Even in a history of the religion of the Turks written in our period there is a passing reference to cabala.[86] To refer to cabala was a form of ostentation among scholars. It established their reputation for being *au courant*.

For our purposes it does not matter whether these erudites believed that important truths could be revealed through cabalistic treatment of the text of the Scriptures. Nor does it matter whether they were ardently opposed to cabala and cabalists. The quest has been for evidences of the diffusion of cabalistic knowledge in the Renaissance, and that knowledge has been found in every type of scholar, everywhere in Europe. From Italy to Scandinavia knowledge of cabala spread. It is perhaps significant that the greater number of those who knew about cabala did not proportionately increase the number who believed in it.

There is one thing more to be said. In every library of any consequence in Europe and in many places in America there are unpublished manuscripts, ranging from fragments of a few leaves to lengthy volumes, dealing with themes brought forward by Pico, Reuchlin, and Agrippa. If ever this vast mine of material should be tapped, it would add considerably to our knowledge of the impact of cabala on the Renaissance mind. Suffice it to say that, even without these manuscript materials, it is evident that the influence of the Christian interpreters of the cabala was, beyond reason, widespread.

[86] Baudier, *Histoire générale de la religion des Turcs*, p. 506.

IX

"AND IN CONCLUSION"

THE MATERIALS which have been presented in previous chapters of this study, although not exhaustive, have pointed to several conclusions which it is the purpose of this section to restate and to emphasize. These conclusions flow from the study itself, rather than from any bias of the student.

It is evident that no single stereotype can describe the Christian interpreters of the cabala. They came from all fields of knowledge, bringing with them inquiring minds marred by an exaggerated respect for authority. They succeeded in creating, for better or for worse, an intellectual situation in which for a time every educated person knew something of the cabala.

The Christian interpreters became interested in cabala and studied it for different reasons. For Pico, cabala was one element in a universal synthetic system of thought. To Reuchlin, cabala was the repository of the lost doctrines of Pythagoras. For Agrippa, cabalism was a prop for an occult system. To Ricci, it was a prime method of converting the Jews. For Thenaud, it was an instrument for the moral instruction and edification of his king. Again, there is no stereotype to cover this variety.

None of the Christian interpreters knew much about the cabala. Ricci, of course, knew most. Even Reuchlin was preëminently indebted to one author. The works of Gikatilia, Recanati's Bible commentary, and the *Book of Formation* practically sum up the knowledge of the interpreters, save Ricci. There was no conception in their minds, or even in the mind of Pistorius at the end of the sixteenth century, of the vastness of Hebrew cabalistic literature.

Yet each thought he had found in the cabala what he was seeking. Some part of the appeal of cabalism must be attributed to this chameleon quality. Each man could derive the aid he sought from its philosophical system, its canons of interpretation, its techniques, or its hermeneutic rules.

Another part of its appeal lay in the fact that the period was transitional in the history of thought. A new sense of the past was developing and, concurrently, a new sense of the future. The old order was changing, but had not yet given place to the new. At such a time, any road looks fair and worthy to be explored.

Of cabala this might well have seemed true more than of most other roads. For cabala had a Hebrew source, and Hebrew was recognized by scholarship of the time as the oldest of languages, as the language of divine revelation. It is by no mere accident that many of those whose names and works have been noticed here were among the pioneer Christian Hebraists. The Christian interpreters of the cabala moved into the field under the impetus to Hebrew learning coming from either humanism, with its concern for language as such, or Biblical studies, with their concern for Hebrew as the language of Scriptures.

Finally, this study has shown an interesting example of the remarkable rapidity with which cultural interests passed from one country to another during the Renaissance. Every corner of Europe knew of and talked of cabala soon after it had been presented in the works of Pico. Without benefit of mechanical means for the diffusion of knowledge, the men of the Renaissance managed to be *au courant*, to be literate in the themes of the moment. For a brief time the Hebrew cabala was one of the themes of the moment, and the Christian interpretation of cabala was born.

APPENDIX A

CORDOVERO

MOSES BEN JACOB CORDOVERO was the author of many cabalistic works; the most important, *Pardes rimmonim* (*A Garden of Pomegranates*), was first printed in Cracow in 1591. Schechter (*Studies in Judaism*, Second Series, p. 240) called the *Pardes* "the clearest and most rational exposition of the Cabbala in existence." The word *Pardes* (*PRDS*) in the title is itself an acrostic of the four senses in which the Torah may be understood: *peshat*, the simple or literal sense; *remez*, the hinting or beckoning sense; *derash*, the homiletical or expository sense; and *sod*, the secret or mystical sense. There is little available literature on Cordovero, especially in English. In addition to the appreciation by Schechter and scattered references in Baron (*History of the Jews*), Graetz (*History of the Jews*), and other such general works, there was nothing of moment until Scholem (*Major Trends in Jewish Mysticism*, pp. 247–51) made a brief statement on Cordovero. A Hebrew crestomathy of Cordovero's writings was compiled by S. A. Horodezky; the selections are not well chosen, and the introduction is of little value.

Generally, the systematic and rational presentation of cabalistic ideas which Cordovero gave to the world has been submerged between the exuberant, lush esotericism of the Zohar, described by Karppe (*Le Zohar*, p. 236) as "du mélange de toutes les tendances les plus divergentes sortira l'œuvre étrange, véritable Babylone des doctrines les plus hautes et les plus puériles: le Zohar," and the theosophy drawn by Vital from the teachings of Isaac Luria of which David Kahana (*A History of the Cabalists*, p. 18) writes very antagonistically in these words: "After the death of R. Moses Cordovero, there came from the hands of R. Chaim Vital . . . [a doctrine] greatly lowering the esteem of Cordovero's cabala, and raising above it a different cabala, the Lurianic. This was, truly, far removed from human reason and logic, and empty of all wisdom and science, full only of suggestions and mysteries, enigmas and superstitions without end." Yet Luria himself was a disciple of Cordovero. It is only fair to state that Scholem (*Major Trends in Jewish Mysticism*, chap. vii) by no means concurs in the unfavorable estimate of the Lurianic cabala to which most of the rationalistic Jewish historians subscribe.

APPENDIX B

WAS RAYMOND LULL A CABALIST?

THE ASCRIPTION of cabalistic views to Lull rests entirely upon the treatise *De auditu kabbalistico; sive, Ad omnes scientias introductorium,* first printed at Venice, 1518. The genuineness of this work was accepted by such students of cabala as Franck (*Kabbalah,* Preface, p. xxxi), and Ginsburg (*Kabbalah,* pp. 83, 199–200); by occultists, such as Westcott (*An Introduction to the Study of the Kabalah,* p. 24) and Levi (*La Clef des grands mystères,* pp. 216–17); by Lullistes such as Asín y Palacios ("Mohhidin," in *Homenaje a Menéndez y Pelayo,* II, 217–56; and *Abenmasarra y su Escuela,* pp. 123–26). Such acceptance led to the torturing of Lull's *Ars magna* to trace its cabalistic basis. This is evident, in epitome, in Stöckl (*Geschichte der Philosophie des Mittelalters,* II, 939):

Es drängt sich hier aber von selbst die Frage auf, wie denn Lullus zu dieser Erfindung seiner "grossen Kunst" gekommen sei. Dass er selbst der Ansicht war, sie durch eine göttliche Offenbarung erhalten zu haben, wissen wir. Das Wahre in dieser Sache dürfte sich daraus ergeben, dass Lullus seine "grosse Kunst" auch als "doctrina sive sapientia *Kabbalistica*" bezeichnet. . . . Allein wir sehen daraus auch, dass Lullus in die jüdische Kabbala wenigstens einigermassen eingeweiht sein musste, weil er Wort und Begriff der Kabbala sich aneignet und auf seine "grosse Kunst" anwendet.

The authenticity of the treatise is now almost universally doubted. Blanco Soto (*Estudios de bibliografía Luliana*) published the three oldest lists of Lull's works. None of them includes *De auditu kabbalistico.* Bové (*El sistema científico Lulliano,* p. 385n) asserts categorically that the treatise is apocryphal. Probst (*Caractère et origine des idées du bienheureux Raymond Lulle (Ramon Lull),* p. 243) says "Le graphisme attribué au Bienheureux ne se trouve

que dans le traité *De Auditu Cabbalistico,* suspect à tous les lullistes
depuis longtemps . . . Il est pour moi, et pour d'autres sans doute,
nettement apocryphe." Littré, in his thorough treatment of Lull
and his work ("Raimond Lulle," in *Histoire littéraire de la France,*
XXIX, 243) presents the case against the treatise in epitome:

(LXXVII) *Ars cabbalistica* ou *Opusculum de auditu cabbalistico.* Cet
opuscule est encore une introduction à l'étude de toutes les sciences. Il
a été souvent imprimé . . . Mais il n'est pas de Raimond. D'abord
l'auteur y cite comme étant son ouvrage un traité *De conditionibus figura-
rum et numerorum,* qu'on ne rencontre nulle part sous le nom de notre
Majorcain; ensuite . . . le langage abstrait de cet *Ars cabbalistica* n'est
pas celui que Raimond parle d'habitude. Enfin, l'ouvrage n'est cité dans
aucun des anciens catalogues. Voilà trois objections dont l'ensemble nous
paraît avoir tout les poids d'un argument décisif.

So decisive, in fact, is the argument against Lull's authorship of
the treatise that Waite (*The Holy Kabbalah,* p. 440), one of the
more scholarly of the recent occultists, is constrained to call "the
treatise entitled De Auditu Kabalistico, an opusculum Raymundinum, or particular application of the method of Lully, which has
been ignorantly included among his works." In the best of the recent
works on Lull (*L'Ars compendiosa de R. Lulle avec une étude sur
la bibliographie et le fond Ambrosien de Lulle,* p. 97), the author,
Carmelo Ottaviano, also considers the treatise apocryphal. Thorndike (*A History of Magic and Experimental Science,* V, 324–25)
tells of having found the manuscript of the treatise (Cod. vatic. lat.
3187) with an ascription to Petrus de Maynardis, whose name appears in its Italian form, Pietro Mainardi, on the title page of the
earliest printed edition. We can, therefore, state categorically that
Lull did not write the treatise and, somewhat hesitantly, that Peter
Maynard did.

APPENDIX C

ARCHANGELUS OF BORGO NUOVO

On the basis of a note in a manuscript used by Steinschneider (*Zeitschrift für hebräische Bibliographie*, II [1897], 94), he suggested that the surname Pozzo, or Puteus, should be added to identify Archangelus. Steinschneider's suggestion was correct as far as it went; a further distinction must, however, be made. Archangelus is not identical with that Aloysius Puteus who was the vicar general of the Franciscan order and the most famous of all the monks of the monastery of Borgo Nuovo (see Wadding, *Annales minorum*, XXI, 272–73).

The man we are seeking to identify was the blood brother of Aloysius Puteus. He is cursorily dismissed by Wadding (*Annales minorum*, XXI, 273) thus: "Habuit eiusdem institute *germanum* fratrem Archangelum *pannosum,* italice *lo stracciato,* ex lacera et segmentate veste, qua ex paupertatis zelo erat indutus, nuncupatum. Summo ingenio praeditus, plura posteris reliquit scripta." Archangelus, in his *Apologia,* listed twenty-one works which he had written. Only four of these have been printed; the rest are in manuscript in European libraries. The printed works show such great dependence on Reuchlin that Scholem (*Bibliographia cabbalistica,* p. 31) refers to one as a plagiary from Reuchlin.

My attention was first directed to this identification by a letter from Bernardinus Aianus to Aloysius Puteus (prefaced to the printing of Archangelus, *Cabalistarum dogmata,* in Pistorius, *Artis cabalisticae scriptores,* p. 731). The letter begins: "Bernardinus Aianus, Reveren. Patri Aloisio Religionis Minoritarum Generali dignissimo, S.P.D. Non ab re futurum duxi, Reverende Pater Aloisi, quid de hoc fratris tui Archangelo libello sentiendum putem, tibi hac epistola significare." Later in the letter, Aianus complains that Archangelus does not have a Ciceronian style. "Phrasin tantum horrebant non admodum Ciceronianam, multaque barbarici, quam latinitati propiora." This criticism is, however, mitigated by praise of Archangelus Puteus as a most learned man.

APPENDIX D

SELECTIONS FROM THENAUD, *LA SAINCTE ET TRESCRESTIENNE CABALE*

(Bibliothèque National manuscrits du Fonds Français, Anciens Fonds, No. 882)

The line numerations in the right-hand margin are not in the original, nor do they represent the structure of the original. They are here introduced to facilitate references from the notes to these selections. The page references in the left-hand margin are those of the original manuscript, and the orthography of the original is preserved unchanged.

[DEDICATION]

Pour nostre tresserenissime Auguste et trescrestien Roy Francoys La aincte et trescrestienne Cabale. metrifiee et mise en ordre par le plus umble de ses serfz Frere Jehan Thenaud. En la quelle sont conenues les sacrees et ierarchalles fontaines de toutes virtuz infuses Ensemble plusieurs secretz de theologie et philozophie.

[PROLOGUE]

O Cler auguste/ et tresserenissime
Roys des francoys/ monarque illustrissime
Sur tous regnans/ portant sceptre inuincible
Pilier de foy/ coulumpne inconcussible. . . .

    .   .   .

Premierement dont de raison cappable   5
Il lauoit fait/ non beste irraisonable.
  Secondement dont sa natiuite
Auoit este en la noble cite
Des atheniens/ ou vraye congnoissance
De dieu/ des cieulx/ de vertuz et science   10

Pouoit auoir/ non en terre barbare
Pays estrange/ ou aultre gent ignare.
  Et tiercement dont il estoit produict
En temps heureux pour pouoir estre instruict
De Socrates philozophe tressage   15
En bonne meurs et scientific vsage.

                    .   .   .

  Le premier est que oultre mauoir fait homme
Il ma donne specialle grace/ en somme
Que procree suis de crestiens parens
En crestiente. Et en temps apparens   20
De seure paix. Si que apres lablution
Du saincte baptesme ay eu instruction
De vraye foy/ et des commandemens
De saincte eglise et de ses sacremens
Et mesmement que de relligion   25
Et ordes sainctz iay eu susception
En angoulmoys vostre pays natif
Qui ma induit tousiours estre ententif
Des parauant vostre natiuite
Prier pour vous que a la prosperite   30
Felicite/ et estat glorieux
Ou ie vous voy peussiez venir. Au mieulx
De mon pouoir. Ce que dieu a permis
Dont los luy rends Et de cueur non remis
Pour tous desirs que sauroys luy requerre   35
Je luy supply faire voller sur terre
Vostre cler nom par renommee telle
Que eureuse fame en vous soit immortelle
  Le second poinct dont ie le remercie
Est de mauoir donner eur en ma vie   40
Que par secours de la superillustre
Qui de vertus sur toutes porte lustre
Plus que palas vostre diuine mere
Qui ma ayde de volunte libere

Paruenu suis a quelque bien sauoir 45
Tant par escriptz/ que pays loingtains veoir
Dont iay bien eu souuent cause et matiere
Tant par prescher quen mainte autre maniere
De a vous parler. Et dauoir assiste
Dauant si saincte et royal maieste 50
Tant lors questiez en florissante enfence
Que regardoys tousiours en excellence
Croistre et fleurir par ampliation
De bruit et los . . .

. . .

Ou mauez fait tout temps commandement 55
De moccuper aux liures visiter
Et a studieux exercice vsiter
Pour vous donner pour occupation
De mes escriptz quelque recreation.
  Et puis le tiers dont luy rends humble grace 60
Cest de mauoir ottroye lieu et place
Dauant voz yeulx pour pouoir presenter
Le petit don quil vous pleut accepter
En si bon vueil et tant begnin courage
Parcydauant de mon debile ouurage 65
Intitule des triumphes morales
Appropriez aux vertus cardinalles
Et dont apres les auoir ouys lire
Et dauant vous/ dhabundant fait relire
Il vous a pleu me commander expres 70
Paracheuer les autres trois empres
A quoy desia iay bien encommence
Continuant mon oeuure. Et auance
Tant que ien suis iusques a esperance
Qui empres dieu en vous seul met ma chance 75
Et luy aydant sire ne cesseray
Que naye fait du mieulx que ie pourray.
  Mais sire/ affin de ma possession

Continuer parfaire oblation
De mon sauoir quoy quil ayt egeste   80
A vostre saincte et royal maieste
Et quelque estrene ou don par chascun an
Vos presenter Qui ne retorque a dain
Jay en brefz motz redige par escript
Selon quay peu Et bien au vray descript   85
La catholicque et tressaincte caballe
Que interpretons/ reception loyalle
Des sacremens absconsez et mussez
Qui reuelez nous sont et adressez
Par foys de dieu/ et des anges aussi   90
Pour paruenir a auoir par cecy
Vraye notice/ et seure congnoissance
De luy et ses separees substances
En tel facon que par layde dicelles
Pourrons fuyr les fraudes et cautelles   95
Des ennemys visifz et inuisibles
Et tous effors malings faulx et nuysibles
Si que viurons en los transquilite
Joye/ repos/ paix/ liesse/ et seurte
On monde bas par contemplation   100
Et on futur par saincte fruition.

    Pareillement sire/ ay mon pouoir mys
Tant que briefte du traicte a permys
A reprouuer caballes vicieuses
Plaines derreurs et supersticieuses   105
Tant des magicz comme des hebrahicques
Autres aussi barbares/ arabicques . . .

       .   .   .

    Vous plaise donc   O tresillustrissime
Roy tressacre/ de cestuy vostre infime
Treshumble serf et pouure pelerin   110
Prendre lestrene/ en cueur doulx et begnin
Ainsi quauez les autres cy dauant

Et lexcuser sil se y treuue souuent
Vice ou erreur. Car en cest art et stille
Ne fut iamais vsite ny abile.   115

. . .

Le vostre serf qui tel la compouse
Nomme Thenaud/ la ainsi diuise
En troys traictez/ sans le prologue y prendre
Dont le premier veult monstrer et apprendre
De paradis maintz merueilleux secretz   120
Et de luy sont Cinq chapitres extraictz.

. . .

En deux protraictz peut lon veoir par expres
Luniuersel puis est monstree apres
Des mondes troys la vraye difference
Et lunion deulx/ par apparence   125
Ce que deduyt le chapitre premier
Du second traict qui est moult singulier.
On second chief lhomme superhabunde
Lequel tout seul faict le quatriesme monde
Et na cy bas certaine demourance   130
Place/ ne lieu/ de seure permanence
Car par vouloir les cieulx peut habiter
Du les enfers si luy plaist heriter.
Mais par autant que cabale que lon dict
Recit celeste ainsi que iay predict   135
Desprit humain ne peut estre anunce
Cestuy present vous sera prononce
Sil plaist a dieu en oracle prospere
De vostre sainct superillustre pere
Prince iadiz tant noble et vertueux   140
A tout le peuple heureux et fructueux
Qui radiant deternel lumiere
Le vous descript en ceste maniere.

[BOOK I, CHAPTER I]

ir   Le celeste oracule et la Cabalistique reuelacion de feu monseigneur au roy son filz En son chastel natif de Compgnac

        Si ores suys auole tout soudain
      Et du hault ciel angelic suzerain
      Ou spirital/ ici bas descendu
      En ce beau lieu que ie esleus de sens dheu
      Pour decorer a mon gre et plaisance   5
      Ta desiree et heureuse naissance
      O mon Chier filz tresflorissante fleur
      Que a present voy couronne en honneur
      Des cleres fleurs de la tige troyanne
      Renouatif et de ma seppe anciene   10
      Pour te informer de lestat glorieux
      On quel ie suys . . .

        .   .   .

      Car tout ainsi que les intelligences
      Que vous nommez angeliques puissances
      Sont transpercens toutz cieulx et elemens   15
      Pour yci bas par saints exhortemens
      Vous inspirer/ sans laisser les haulz cieulx:
      Et que le rays du soleil lumineux
      Ou les influx des planetes descendent/
      Et leur clarte en ce bas monde rendent   20
      En vng instant par puissance effectiue
      Sans delaisser leur source primitiue
      En laquelle ont imperceptiblement
      Leur brief retour. Ainsi ay promptement
      Faict. Et ce font/ quant il leur plaist le faire   25
      Mes bienheurez concitoiens de gloire.

        .   .   .

iv   Premierement saches que le hault dieu
      Seul dieu des dieux qui domine en tout lieu

Qui de beaulte verite indicible
Et de bonte est font incomprehensible . . .   30

.   .   .

iv–iir   Voulut creer mon ame nette et pure
Immaculee/ et sans tache ou ordure
Franche/ libere/ et vertible.

.   .   .

iir   Ayant esgard seulement soyes seur
Premier a toy/ puys a ta diue seur   35
Qui seulz estiez aueques vostre mere
Superillustre/ et miene espouse chere. . . .

.   .   .

iiv   Par ces deux pointz de iustice et pitie
Ie aquiz de dieu la grace et amytie
Et transuolay ainsi que avec deux helles   40
La sus es cieulx aux ioyes supernelles.
Ce ne fut pas sans secours de mon ange
Et bon esprit/ qui ne me fut estrange
Mais seur ducteur/ car des trosnes glorieux
Ierarque estoit/ qui tant sont precieux   45
Cil me logea lassus en sondit orde
Vng second iour si bien ie men recorde
Que on disoit mil quatre cens quatre vingts
Et seze auec/ que on ciel empire vins
On quel trouuay plusieurs de mes ancestres   50
Roys empereurs portans glorieux sceptres.

.   .   .

iiir–v   O ma royalle et diue geniture
Ie te diroys voluntiers et te asseure
Et monstreroys de la felicite
Et souuerain bien de la haulte cite   55
Ou ie demeure en perdurable gloire

Pour quen eusses continue memoire
Et soubuenir. Mais le vueil supernel
Piteuse grace et amour paternel
Ne lont voulu et ne voulent permettre   60
Acelle fin de non te induyre ou mettre
En triste soing ou en profond penser
Qui te pourroient causer et adroisser
Mepris moult grand de tes florissans iours   65
Par quoy perdroys tes plus plaisans seiours.

.   .   .

iii*v*–iv*r*   A quelquesfoys que te verras seulet
Et solitayre en ton beau cabinet
Saincte et secret Eslieue tes espritz
Si haultement/ que par eulx soient compriz
De tous les cieulx la spaciosite   70
Des planettes la speciosite
Le firmament et le premier mobile
Dict cristalin/ que aulcun tant fust habile
Des anciens philozophes iamais
Ne transcendit/ Encore contemple/ mais   75
Leur mouuemens diuers et merueilleux
Les vngs heureux les aultres perilleux
Les vngs ayans figures ecentriques
Aultres tournans en droictz poinctz concentriques.
Pareillement voy leurs innumerables   80
Raiz cours/ vertuz et puissances muables
Signes influx et leurs tours et leurs lieux
Que trouueras adiustez par trop myeulx
Que ne scauroit compas geometric
Ne nombre aulcun supermathematic   85
Lors ton esprit si tresenlumine
Quant de ce aura este en doctrine
Vouldra scauoir qui est ce hault pouoir
Qui tous ces corps faict en ce point mouuoir

Et dont ilz ont leurs beaultez ou vertuz
Et proprietez dont ilz sont reuestuz.

.   .   .

[CHAPTER 2]

vr   Le premier et incomprehensible triangle de la diuine gloire.
vr–v   Or par dessus celles intelligences
          Que tay nommez angeliques essences
          Est leternelle et diuine nature
          En sa bonte/ supreme et sans mesure/
          Purement pure/ et toute deifique   5
          Estant en estre/ vniquement vnique/
          Infiniment infime beaute/
          Absolument absolue verite/
          Puissant pouoir/ puissant forme omniforme
          Formellement formelle sans difforme/   10
          Qui est par tout indiuisiblement
          Et oultre tout essenciallement.
          A qui tous cas et dictz affirmatifz
          Et negatifz/ positifz/ priuatifz
          Quelconques sont/ et ceulx qui point ne sont   15
          Soient entenduz/ ou qui ententes nont
          Contrarians/ ou que on peut impugner
          Ou repugner/ pouons atribuer:
          Pour veu pourtant que en leur diffinicion
          Nemportent mal ny imperfection.   20

.   .   .

vv–vir   Ainsi apert le merueilleux et sainct
          Sacre mistere en mon recit succint
          De la benoiste et saincte trinite
          Qui ne pourroit estre a la verite
          Sceu tel quil est en son ens souuerain   25
          Fors de son entendement primerain
          Qui congnoissant et soy et son essence

Par seul vouloir/ et diuine puissance
En se voyant/ congnoist et a cler voit
Ce qui doibt estre au parauant quil soit   30
Et toute chose estant ores presente
Le quel scauoir est cause efficiente
De donner germe et generacion
Entendement estre et perfection
A toutes et chascunes creatures   35
Passees soient presentes ou futures.

.   .   .

viv   Et ia soit or quil nest entendement
Sens ne scauoir qui sceust aulcunement
Bien figurer la maieste diuine
Vne en essence et en personne trine   40
Qui oultrepasse tout ens et figure
Infiniment/ aussi toute nature
Ce neaumoins pour que a icelle puisses
Sureleuer par diuins artifices
De ton esprit la haulte porcion   45
Si ten donray significacion
Tant seullement on point indiuisible
Triangulair de gloire incomprehensible.

.   .   .

[CHAPTER 3]

viiv   Du second triangle dict le triangle de triumphe on quel
sont les Seraphins Cherubins et Trosnes/ et les sources de Charite
Prudence et Justice. . . .

.   .   .

En celuy sont premier les seraphins
Les cherubins/ puys les trosnes diuins
Esqueulx ainsi que es obiectz principaulx   ̣ɔ
De toutz creez plus esleuez et haultz. . . .

.   .   .

Ensemble vnist sans quelque aultre mixtion   5
Lamour susdict eternel incree
A lautre amour seraphic et cree.

    .   .   .

viii*r*   De ce second triangle ierarchique
Troys beaux ruisseaux de source manifique
Vienent sortir/ dont le premier prouient   10
De charite/ qui des seraphins vient.
Lautre en apres est produit par Prudence
Des cherubins/ Et le tiers prend naissance
Du cler conduict des trosnes par iustice
Et equite qui a tous est propice.   15

    .   .   .

viii*r–v*   Mais par amour eternel et non rudde
Quil a voulu a toutz distribuer
Et fermer paix permanent sans muer
A toutz creez a faict communicance
Au quadranglet deternelle aliance   20
Car comme vng feu lautre feu a soy tire
En ce quadrant lune amour lautre attire
Qui des trians de triumphe et de gloire
Vient resulter/ comme en proctait notoire
Veoir le pourraz . . .   25

    .   .   .

viii*v–*ix*r* Saches encor pour vng point singulier
Que cil amour susdict quadrangulier
Faisant de soy communication
En cinq amours recoit diuision
Premierement est son amour diuin . . .   30
    Lautre amour est angelic . . .
    Le tiers amour est spirituel . . .
    Et par le quart quest amour animal . . .
    Le cinquiesme est purement naturel . . .

    .   .   .

ixv–xr   O royal lys/ congnoys que pour troys raisons   35
Ont nom de feu pour iustes comparaisons.
La premiere est car ainsi que le feu monte . . .
    Lautre est que ainsi que feu materiel . . .
    Et tiercement comme le feu actif
Est purgatif/ et illuminatif   40
Quant sa lueur les tenebres dechasse
Semblablement les seraphims ont grace
De illuminer toutz les inferieurs
Par leur clartes et splendidans lueurs
Et les parfaire et purger de nescience   45
Dautant quilz ont plus haulte congnoissance
Des grands tresors et misteres diuins
Par le moyen dessusdictz seraphins.

       .   .   .

xir   Les cheurubins qui glorieusement
Et sans moyen/ voyent en dieu/ et congnoissent   50
Ses grands secretz/ et tresors/ point ne cessent
De contempler sa haulte sapience . . .

       .   .   .

xiv   Le tiers canton du triumphe susdict
Qui tierce spere intellectuelle est dict
Font en apres les trosnes glorieux   55
Qui ont leur nom au semblabe de ceulx
Esquelz les roys et les gouuernemens
Scent et font leurs mondains iugemens
Lesqueulx sont haultz et sur terre esleuez
Stables/ ornez/ et noblement parez   60
De fins tapiz dyaprez et couuers
A receuoir leur sieur tousiours ouuers . . .

       .   .   .

xiiv   O que heureux sont excellens glorieux
Sainctz et sacres dignes et precieux

Les triumphans aueque le victeur 65
Dieu supernel puissant/ triumphateur
On trianglet de triumphe eternel
Et sont viuans au regne supernel
De sainct amour/ equite/ sapience
Par le vouloir du pere/ et la puissance 70
Du filz/ aussi lamour du sainct esprit/
Esqueulx tout bien resplendist et reluyt.

. . .

[CHAPTER 4]

xiii*r*   Du tiers triangle dict de Victoire qui font les anges de la
seconde ierarchie dictz les potestes/ principautez et dominacions.
Duquel yst et sort Force/ Temperance et Humilite.

. . .

xiiii*v*   Et par ainsi les anges superieurs
Toutes graces ont des inferieurs
Car les haultz ont seigneurie et puissance
Sans elacion ou aulcune arrogance
Les inferieurs sont aussi par droicture 5
Obeissans sans desdaing ou murmure.

. . .

Et ia soit que ames/ soient spirituelles
Comme anges sont ce neaumoins entre elles
Ya moult grand difference/ Car lange
Ne soy vnist iamais a corps estrange 10
Comme feroit la matiere a la forme
Dont en ce nest lame a luy conforme.
Lange aussi est pur intellectuel
Pour ce entend il et par droit naturel
Scet et congnoist de seul regard immuable; 15
Mais lame estant seulement raisonnable
Nentend que par sillogizacions/

Discours et temps/ et les conclusions
Scet et comprend seulement des premisses.

. . .

xviir   Aulcuns ont dict que ceste ierarchie   20
Tout aultrement que dessus officie
Car les premiers droissent les actions
Des anges/ et leurs operacions
Et les seconds les maiestez et princes
A gouuerner et regir leurs prouinces   25
Et que les tiers excercent leurs pratiques
A reprimer les assaultz dyaboliques.   •

[CHAPTER 5]

xviir   Du derrier et bas triangle de glorieuse deffence et vertueux combat/ qui font les vertuz archanges et anges pour le secours
des ames raisonnables/ qui sont on champ de bataille. Des radieuses
fontaines de Foy Perseuerance et obeissance. Et la figure de toutes
les celestes ierarchies.

. . .

xviiv   Par ainsi est basty/ edifie
Et asseure construict fortifie
Le quadrangle dasseurance et esbat
Par les trians de victoire et combat
Comme est celuy de charite notoyre   5
Par les trians de triumphe et de gloire
Desqueulx lon voit que les fondemens font
Des triangles/ et quadrangles damont
Troys simples tretz Qui font en cest affaire
Representer par leur nombre ternaire   10
Que la celeste armee nest de soy
Cheualeureuse Mais fondee en la foy
De trinite superimperialle.
     Les plus haulte traict ou ligne principalle
Dor/ represente et pour vray signifie   15

De trinite la haulte monatchie
Et la plus basse en raison bien notable
Noire prinse est pour lame raisonnable
Laquelle on rang des formes naturelles
Pareillement des intellectuelles   20
Qui peuent auoir congnoissance de dieu
Tient le plus bas et plus infime lieu
Dont pour icelle enuers les ennemys
Deffendre mieulx/ sont les bons anges mys
Et ordonnez en puissante bataille   25
Prestz dayder sil conuient quon assaille
Par ce doibt lon lever a mont ses yeulx
Deuotement en disant a iceulx
Nunc in montes occulos leuaui
Vnde veniet auxilium michi   30

.   .   .

[BOOK II, CHAPTER I]

xxiii*r*   Des troys mondes cestassauoir angelic/ celeste/ et elementaire qui ne font fors vng mond.

Or mon chier filz roy tresserenissime
Entendre peuz ainsi que ie lextime
Par ce quay dit/ es susdictes parolles
Qui vrayes sont non songes ne friuolles
Des mondes trois . . .   5

.   .   .

Dont le premier quay dit intelligible
Ou angelic/ de clarte indicible
Est tout remply et dangelicques formes
Plaines de gloire en nulles pars difformes
Qui le parfont/ tout beau oultre mesure   10
Sans quantite sans matiere ou figure
Et ne sauroit leur nombre aucun compter
Car plus aise seroit de racompter

Quantz gouttes a dedens la mer profunde
Ou de flambeaux en tout la sphere ronde   15
Du firmament. Qui sont en ierarchie
Tous adorans le terne monarchie
Aussi stables sans aucun mouement
Oultrepassans lestelle firmament.

xxiiir–v   Le second est dict celeste et mobile   20
Tousiours tournant sans en estre debile
Sur les deux polz/ lung denomme articque
Lautre opposit appelle antarticque
Qui icelluy tiennent ainsi que essieux
Et est aussi diuise en neuf cieulx   25
En cestuy sont les influans planettes
Astres luysans et les estelles nettes
Si est regy par le superieur
Et de luy est regy linferieur
Auquel transmet raiz chaleur et lumiere   30
Oultrepercant des terres le miniere.

xxiiiv–   Le tiers plus bas est dit elementaire
xxivr   Onquel est clos celluy palus notoire
Noir stigieux/ qui par ses ardens cours
Neuf cercles fait es infernaulx decours   35
Manoir de mort/ plain de corruption
Dennuy/ labeur/ pleur/ alteration
De dueil soucy souspir et gref misere
Trop plus que icy ne te dis ou refere
Icelluy est variable instabile   40
Materiel corruptible et mobile
Qui porte en soy toutes choses confuses
Et en abiect mussees et recluses
A subiecty a ruynes temporelles
Par decadence/ Et des spirituelles   45
Moult eslongne et par longue distance
Mais toutesfois sans quelque resistance
Il obeist come matiere a forme

Car son cahos seroit par trop difforme
Et non obstant ladicte difference   50
Lung a lautre est en durable aliance
Duy et ioinct par vng commun accord
Si que linflux qui des haultz vient et sort
Est mieulx receu que du passif lactif
Ou que le germe en forme sensitif   55
En tel facon que ce quest en lung deulx
Se treuue tout/ es autres mondes deux
Quoy quil soit mieulx et plus parfaictement
Es suserains qui sont sans mouuement
Sauoir pourras par exemplarite   60
De mon recit la pure verite.

   Icy bas est au monde elementaire
Le feu duquel vous auez luminaire
Puis est ou ciel le cler soleil luysant
Du monde loeil moult utile et duysant   65
Mais plus hault sont les ardens seraphins
Plus lumineux que escarboncles tresfins
Chascun desquelz en son monde sapplicque
A bien ouurer sans seiour ou repplicque
Lung est brullant Le second viuifie   70
Et puis le tiers en amour beatifie
Les bons espritz qui sont purifiez
Immaculez de vices nettiez.

   De rechef est cy bas leau froide et moitte
La lune on ciel/ qui par nature humecte   75
Puis audessus sapience cherubine
Luysante en qui toute ymage tresfine
Se cause et fait de raisons eternelles
Come en fine eau mirons noz faces belles.

   Or nest il riens en ce monde parfond   80
Qui nay estoille au ciel serein amont
Et par dessus son ydee exemplaire
Que prouidence en voulant tout parfaire

A estably et ainsi ordonne
Tant au produict come a ce qui est ne. 85

. . .

[CHAPTER 2]

xxiiiiv Du quart monde qui est lhomme.
    Oultre ces trois le quart miraculeux
Microcosme est/ qui na forme ne lieux
Propres a soy mais tel quil vouldra estre
Il se fera. Ce quautres dez leur naistre
Faire ne peuent/ ne usurper autre lieu 5
Ne forme/ fors celle que a pleu a dieu
Leur ottroyer/ dez quilz furent creez.
Poisson ne vit es terres labourees
Ne aussi loizeau en bas come vne vache
Aussi poissons ne mettons a lattache 10
Pour les muher en cerfz ou arondelles
Car ilz nauront iamais iambes ny heles
Pour bas courir/ ou en laer voltiger
Mais leur conuient tousiours en eau nager.
xxiiiiv–   Beste nya tant soit or precieuse 15
xxvr Tant gracieuse et doulce ou venimeuse
Qui viure sceust on pur vif element
Du feu qui art et brusle clerement
Ainsi que fait le royal salamendre
Qui luy resiste et nen est pire ou mendre 20
Ains le destruict en succent sa chaleur
Soy promenant en sa flambe et ardeur.
Mais lhomme humain qui en ses trois parties
Du corps entier/ sans estre departies
Lymage fait des trois dessusditz mondes 25
Les formes prend/ soient belles ou immundes
Telles quil veult . . .

. . .

xxvi*r*   Pour que tel don/ soit donc donne a lhomme
Il est besoing quil soit tout ainsi comme
Desprit rauy/ furieux/ enyure   30
De sainct amour Et quil soit deliure
Damour mondain/ et de passions viles/
Et que vertuz purgatoires/ ciuiles/
Soient en luy/ et desperit purge.
Semblablement et quil soit repurge   35
Par sacremens et contemplations
En reprimant ordes emotions.

[CHAPTER 3]

xxvi*r*   Icy est reprouuee la cabale supersticieuse.

      .   .   .

xxvii*v*   Par quel marche furent faitz les recors
Cy dauant ditz/ et hereticz accors
Des diuers sors/ formes et caracteres
Furent iamais patriarches notaires
Ou tabellions de toutes ces follies   5
Qui ont les ditz et lectres amollies
Non seulement de la philozophie
Mais de la saincte et vraye theologie
Attribuans leur supersticions
Curieux escriptz et vaines fictions   10
A salomon/ aussi a daniel
Enos esdraz/ mathie et samuel.
Moyse font de magicque le prince . . .

      .   .   .

xxviii*v*–   Si les hebreux auoient telle puissance
xxix*r*   Par leurs escriptz et antique science   15
De quoy leur sert/ veu que a execution
Mise ne lont en la vexation
Exil/ prisons/ et dure seruitude

Quilz ont soubstins en forte amaritude
Par si long traict et espace de temps   20
Sans eulx tenir on mespris et contemps
De tout le monde et en serf saufconduit
En leur sauoir a donc peu de desduit
Sil sest iadis fait en leur sinagogue
Miracle ainsi que leglise emologue   25
Come il aduint dedans la rouge mer
Que fit moyse ouurir et entamer
Dauoir la manne a tous goustz sauoureuse
Ou retourner/ par oraison piteuse
Le cler soleil/ de son cours ordinaire   30
Par iosue duc preux et de bonaire
Et autres maintz dont ne fais mention
Soit regarde au vray sans fiction
Si le recit des sainctes escriptures
Approuue point que lettres ou figures   35
Leur ayent seruy de riens en tout cecy
Certes nenny croyez le donc ainsi.

. . .

xxixr–v   Ceste estoit bien digne reception
Cabale saincte/ et reuelation
Qui ne vouloit caracteres friuoles/   40
Cerues sphericz/ ne lectres ne simboles/
Mais seulement iustice/ et equite
Foy charite/ zele/ amour/ purite/
Obseruation des sainctz commandemens.

. . .

[CHAPTER 4]

xxixv   La vraye et saincte cabale. Aussi qui sont les vrays cabalistes.
xxixv–   Ainsi pourront estre ditz cabalistes
xxxr   Les crestiens qui les euangelistes
Bien receuront Et ce que nostre dieu

En ce bas monde a presche en maint lieu
Non pas anunce par prophetes obscurs   5
En leurs sermons/ ne par signes confus
Mais par lorgane et bouche de son filz
Comme tu croys mon tresodorant lys/
Et qui aussi dignement perceuront
Les sacremens/ par lesquelz gousteront   10
Des bons espritz les souefues delices
Qui proprement ne sont que es saincts propices
Et mesmement cil de leurcaristie
Qui spirituel feu embrase ou auye
Dedans celle ame/ en qui est charite   15
Dont la clarte rend viue immensite.

.   .   .

[BOOK III, CHAPTER I]

xxxi*r*   Comment le monde intellectuel ou angelic influe on second
celeste lequel il regist et gouuerne.

.   .   .

xxxi*v*   Le premier est dit/ simple simplement
Qui ne permet en soy aucunement
De nombre aultruy la composition
Solitaire est en apprehension
Illimite/ et incomprehensible   5
Qui a dieu seul tout puissant indicible
Est ottroye. Lequel point ne confond
De trinite le mistere profund
Ne lunite ne destruit trinite
Veu que la est totalle equalite   10
Dessence et bien/ de beaulte et puissance
De loyaulte/ amour/ et sapience.
    Le second est nombre simple denaire
Le tetractis/ ou bien le quaternaire
Philozophal/ qui est source profunde   15
Ou le compose bien afferme et prou funde

Nombre infim dont multitude pend
Qui en tous lieux et oultre tous se expend
Mais dudit nombre lunite ne recoit
Composicion/ quelconque quelle soit   20
Ne aucun mixtion/ par ce que cest le terne
Qui est par tout tousiours vnique et terne
Tant par pouoir/ que presence et essence
Aultrement est riens luniuersal sans ce
Pour ce de soy faisant communion   25
Par saincte amour/ il donne en vnion.

· · ·

xxxii*r–v*   Si doys sauoir que tous les noms des anges
Qui reuelez nous sont/ et des archanges
Sont terminez/ en yah/ on en el
Signifians que le dieu eternel   30
Est iuste/ et tout misericordieux
Aussi bailloient iadis les romains tieulx
Epithetons de appeller/ optimus
Leur iupiter et aussi/ maximus.
    Les tiers nombre est dit mixte ou compose   35
Moult differant de cil dont iay ose
Cy te enseigner les grandes proprietez
De leur nature aussi les varietez
Car du simple est lunite increee
Et nest de luy composition creee   40
Aussi sont ceulx dicelluy fix et stables
Non conuertis a ces choses muables
Ainsi que sont estoilles et planettes
Mais quant de leurs intelligences nectes
Elles en dieu sont si profund rauies   45
Que des corps nont cures soings ny enuies
Bien noz espritz et ames luy addressent
Et on chemin de paradis nous dressent
Mais lunite des nombres composez
Si est creee/ aussi sont disposez   50

A soy conioindre/ et par bonne alliance
Les cieulx regir et donner linfluence
Qui en cestuy bas monde elementaire
Char et produict tout ce quest neccessaire.

[CHAPTER 2]

.   .   .

[CHAPTER 3]

.   .   .

[CHAPTER 4]

.   .   .

[CHAPTER 5]

.   .   .

[CHAPTER 6]

.   .   .

[CHAPTER 7]

.   .   .

[EPILOGUE]

.   .   .

liii*r*   Dieu tout puissant qui seul cree et procree
        Tous les espritz A ton ame creee
        Vingt cinq ans a come bien le remembre
        Et fut vng iour douziesme de septembre . . .

               .   .   .

lviii*r*   Or mon amy trescher filz precieux   5
        Presentement suis euoque des cieulx
        Pour retourner en mon siege de gloire
        Et te laisser en triumphant victoire
        Ou demourras et en felicite
        Jusques a ce que seras sus cite   10
        De ce bas monde et siecle terrien
        Et que le tien esprit soit ioinct au mien
        En la clarte de gloire lumineuse
        Sans separer et pour iamais eureuse.

BIBLIOGRAPHY

HEBREW SOURCES

Anatoli, Jacob, Ruah hen [The Spirit of Grace]. Berlin, 1931.

Cordovero, Moses, Pardes rimmonim [A Garden of Pomegranates]. Cracow, 1591.

[De Leon, Moses], Sefer ha-zohar [Book of Splendor]. Lublin, 1872.

—— The Zohar; English translation by Sperling and Simon. London, 1931–34.

—— Sepher ha-Zohar (Le Livre de la splendeur); doctrine ésotérique des Israélites; French translation by Jean de Pauly. Paris, 1906–11.

Gikatilia, Joseph, Sha'are orah [The Gates of Light]. Lemberg, 1858.

Herrera, Abraham Cohen, Shaar ha-shamayim [The Gate of Heaven]. Warsaw, 1864.

Jellinek, Adolph, Auswahl kabbalistischer Mystik. Part I, Leipzig, 1853.

Macgregor Mathers, S.L., The Kabbalah Unveiled. London, 1887.

Recanati, Menahem, Perush al ha-Torah [Commentary on the Torah]. Venice, 1523.

Ricci, Paul, tr., Portae lucis; hec est porta tetragrammaton iusti intrabunt per eam. Augsburg, 1516.

Scholem, Gerhard G., ed., Das Buch Bahir. Leipzig, 1923. Kabbala; Quellen und Forschungen zur Geschichte der jüdischen Mystik, Vol. I.

Sefer Raziel ha-moloch [The Book of the Angel Raziel]. Wilna, 1881.

Stenring, Knut, ed. and tr., The Book of Formation (Sepher Yetzirah). London, 1923.

CHRISTIAN INTERPRETATIONS OF THE CABALA

In the attempt to make this listing as complete as possible I have included many books not consulted in the preparation of this study. These are indicated by an asterisk.

Abramus, Nicolaus, S.J., Pharus veteris testamenti sive sacrarum quaestionum, libri xv, quibus accesserunt eiusdem authoris De veritate et mendacio, libri iv. Paris, 1648.

Agrippa, Henry Cornelius, Opera; in duos tomos concinne digesta, et nunc denuo sublatis omnibus mendis in philomuson gratiam accuratissime recusa. Lyons, 1532.

—— Three Books of Occult Philosophy [English translation by J.F.]. London, 1651.

Albinius, P. Constantius, Magia astrologica. Paris, 1611.*

Allix, Peter, The Judgment of the Ancient Jewish Church against the Unitarians in the Controversy upon the Holy Trinity and the Divinity of Our Blessed Saviour. Oxford, 1821.

Alting, Jacob A., "De cabbala scripturaria," in Opera, Vol. V, Amsterdam, 1687.

Amama, Sixtius, Anti-barbarus biblicus. Franeker, 1656.*

Anania, Johannes L., De natura daemonum, libri iv. Venice, 1589.

Andreä, Samuel, Examen generale cabbalae philosophicae Henrici Mori. Herborn, 1670.*

Aquinas, Philip, Interprétation de l'arbre de la cabale. Paris, 1625. Reimpression, Paris, 1906.

—— Veterum rabbinorum in exponendo Pentateucho modi tredecim. Paris, 1620.

Bacon, Francis, The New Atlantis. London, 1631.

—— Of the Advancement and Proficiencie of Learning. Oxford, 1640.

Baudier, Michel, Histoire générale de la religion des Turcs. Auvergne, 1641.

Belot, Jean, Les Fleurs de la philosophie chrestienne et morale; ou, Refutations de Henry Cor. Agrippa et de P. d'Abano en leur philosophie occulte. Paris, 1603.

—— Instruction familière et très facile pour apprendre les sciences de chiromancie et phisiognomie. Paris, 1619.

Benedictus, Joannes, De visionibus et revelationibus naturalibus et divinis libellus elegans ac compendiosus. Mayence, 1550.*

Bernegger, M., Orationes duae de cabbala. Strassburg, 1640.*

Bongus, Petrus, Mysticae numerorum significationis. Bergamo, 1585.

Borch, Olaf, Dissertatio de kabala characterali. Copenhagen, 1699.*

Bruno, Giordano, De monade numero et figure, in Opera latine conscripta, ed. F. Fiorentino. Naples, 1879–91, Vol. I.

Bullinger, Henry, The Decades. Cambridge, 1851. Parker Society Publications, Vol. XLII.

Burnet, Thomas, Archaeologia philosophica; sive, Doctrina antiqua de rerum originibus libri ii. London, 1692.

Buxtorf, Johannes, the Elder, Synagoga Iudaica: hoc est, schola Iudae-
orum, in quo nativitas, institutio, religio, vita, mors, sepulturaque
ipsorum e libris eorundem descripta est. Hanau, 1604.
Buxtorf, Johannes, the Younger, De abbreviaturis Hebraicis. Herborn,
1708.
—— Tractatus de punctorum, vocalium et accentuum in libris veteris
testamenti Hebraicis, origine, antiquitate et authoritate, oppositus Ar-
cano punctationis revelato Ludovici Cappelli. Basel, 1648.
Cabalae verior descriptio, d.i., Beschreibung aller natürlichen und über-
natürlichen Dingen, wie durch das Verbum Fiat alles erschaffen, und
darnach durch das Centrum Coeli et Terrae generirt wird. Hamburg,
1680.
Cappellus, Ludovicus, Arcanum punctationis revelatum; sive, De punctorum vocalium et accentuum apud Hebraeos vera et germana antiquitate diatriba. Leyden, 1624.
—— De veris et antiquis Ebraeorum literis. Amsterdam, 1645.
Carpzov, J. Benedict, Apparatus historico-criticus antiquitatum sacri
codicis et gentis Hebraeae: uberrimis annotationibus in Thomas Good-
wini Mosen et Aaronem. Frankfort, 1748.
—— Introductio in theologiam Judaicam, in Martin, Raymond, Pugio
Fidei. Leipzig, 1687.
Carretus, Ludovicus, "Epistola de conversione eius ad Christum, ex
Hebraeo Latine conversa. 1553," in Buxtorf, Johannes, the Elder,
Synagoga Iudaica. Hanau, 1604, pp. 596–644.
Champier, Symphorien, Pronosticon libri iii. Lyons, 1518.*
Cheradamus, Joannes, Alphabetum linguae sanctae mystico intellectu
refertum. Paris, 1532.*
Chrisogonus, Federicus, De modo collegiandi pronosticandi et curandi
febres: necnon de humana felicitate ac denique de fluxu et refluxu
maris lucubrationes. Venice, 1528.*
Cigogna, Strozzius, Magiae omnifariae, vel potius, universae naturae
theatrum. Cologne, 1606.
Colet, John, Letters to Radulphus on the Mosaic Account of the Crea-
tion; ed. with an English translation by J. H. Lupton. London, 1876.
—— Two Treatises on the Hierarchies of Dionysius; ed. with an English translation by J. H. Lupton. London, 1869.
Collange, Gabriel, Dissertatio de cabala; appended to Tritheim, Poly-
graphia. Translated into French by Gabriel Collange. Paris, 1561.
Constantinus, Robert, Nomenclator insignium scriptorum. Paris, 1555.*

Copus, M., Cabala, speculum artis et naturae in alchymia. [Augsburg], 1654.

Crispus, Johannes Baptista, De Platone caute legendo . . . libri xxiii. Rome, 1594.

Croll, Oswald, Basilica chimica. Frankfort, 1609.

Cudworth, Ralph, The True Intellectual System of the Universe. London, 1820.

Cunaeus, Petrus, De republica Hebraeorum libri iii. Rome, 1666.

Dee, John, Monas hieroglyphica mathematice, cabalistice, anagogiceque explicata, in Zetzner, Lazarus, ed., Theatrum chemicum, II (Strassburg, 1659), pp. 178–215.

Della Riviera, Cesare, Il magico mondo de gli heroi. Mantua, 1603.

Del Rio, Martin, S.J., Disquisitionum magicarum libri vi. Cologne, 1679.

De Mornay, Philip, A Work concerning the Trewnesse of the Christian Religion. Translated into English by Sir Philip Sidney and Arthur Golding. London, 1604.

De Nuysement, Jacques, Tractatus de vero sale secreto philosophorum et de universali mundi spiritu. Cassell, 1651.

De Tyard, Pontus, L'Univers; ou, Discours des parties et de la nature du monde. Lyons, 1557.

D'Evoli, Cesare, De divinis attributis quae sephirot ab Hebraeis nuncupantur. Venice, 1589.

Digby, Everard, Theoria analytica viam ad monarchiam scientiarum demonstrans. London, 1579.

Dorneus, Gerard, Congeries Paracelsicae chemiae de transmutationibus metallorum, in Zetzner, Lazarus, ed., Theatrum chemicum, I (Strassburg, 1613), pp. 533–619.

Duret, Claude, Thrésor de l'histoire des langues de cest únivers. Cologne, 1613.

Elisius, Joannes, Satis metuendi diluvii verissima liberatio. Bologna, 1522.*

Erastus, Thomas, Disputationis de medicina nova P. Paracelsi. Pars altera. [Basel], 1572.

Fabricius, Laurentinus, De schem hamphorasch usu, et abusu apud Iudaeos, orationes duae. Wittenberg, 1596.

Fisher, John, The English Works. Part I. London, 1876. Early English Text Society, Extra Series, No. XXVII.

Fliscus, Mauritius, Decas de fato, annisque fatalibus tam hominibus quam regnis mundi. Frankfort, 1665.

Fludd, Robert, Sophiae cum moria certamen, in quo lapis Lydius a falso structore Fr. Marino Mersenno, celeberrima voluminis sui Babylonici figmenta accurate examinata. Frankfort, 1629.

—— Summum bonum, quod est verum subjectum verae Magiae, Cabalae, Alchymiae. Frankfort, 1629.

—— Mosaicall Philosophy, Grounded upon the Essential Truth or Eternal Sapience. London, 1659.

Frommann, Johann, Tractatus de fascinatione novus et singularis. Nuremberg, 1675.

Gaffarel, Jacques, Abdita divinae cabalae mysteria, contra sophistarum logomachiam defensa. Paris, 1625.

—— Codicum cabbalisticorum manuscriptorum quibus est usus Ioannes Picus, comes Mirandulanus index. Paris, 1651.

—— Curiositez inouyes, sur la sculpture talismanique des Persans; horoscope des patriarches; et lecture des estoilles. n.p., 1650.

Galatinus, Petrus, De arcanis catholicae veritatis contra obstinatissimam Judaeorum nostrae tempestatis perfidiam. Bari, 1516.

Garzonus, Thomas, La Piazza universale di tutte le professioni del mondo e nobili et ignobili nuovamente formata e portata in luce. Venice, 1588.

Génin, F., L'Eclaircissement de la langue française par Jean Palsgrave, suivi de la Grammaire de Giles du Guez. Paris, 1852.

Georgius, Franciscus, De harmonia mundi totius cantica tria. Venice, 1525.

Godelmann, Johann Georg, De magis veneficiis et lamiis recte cognoscendis et puniendis libri iii. Frankfort, 1591.*

Godwyn, Thomas, Moses and Aaron: Civil and Ecclesiastical Rites Used by the Ancient Hebrews. 9th ed. London, 1667.

Gohorry, Jacques, Theophrasti Paracelsi philosophiae et medicinae utriusque universae compendium. Paris, n.d.*

Gretser, Jacobus, S.J., De iure et more prohibendi, expurgandi, et abolendi libros haereticos et noxios. Ingolstadt, 1603.

Guinther of Andernach, J., De medicina veteri et nova. Basel, 1571.*

Hackspan, Theodor, Miscellaneorum sacrorum libri ii, quibus accessit ejusdem exercitatio de cabbala Judaica. Altdorf, 1660.

Henning, Johann, Cabbalologia; sive, Brevis institutio de cabbala cum veterum rabbinorum Judaica tum poëtarum paragrammatica. Leipzig, 1683.

Hoogstraten, Jacob, Apologia ad Leon P.M. contra dialogum in cause Reuchlin scriptum. Cologne, 1518.*

—— Destructio cabalae seu cabalistice perfidie ab J. Reuchlin capnione in lucem edite. Cologne, 1519.

Hoornbeeck, Johannes, Summa controversiarum religionis. Utrecht, 1653.

—— Teshubat Yehudah; sive, Pro convincendis et convertendis Judaeis libri viii. Leyden, 1655.

Horn, George, Historiae philosophicae libri vii quibus de origine, successione, sectis et vita philosophorum ab orbe condito ad nostram aetatem agitur. Leyden, 1655.

Hottinger, Joh. Henricus, Promtuarium; sive, Bibliotheca orientalis. Heidelberg, 1658.

Howard, Henry, Earl of Northampton, A Defensative against the Poyson of Supposed Prophecies. London, 1620.

Justinianus, Augustinus, Precatio pietatis plena ad DEUM omnipotentem composita ex duobus et septuaginta nominibus divinis Hebraicis et Latinis una cum interprete commentariola. [Venice (?)], 1513.

—— Psalterium Hebraeum, Graecum, Arabicum, et Chaldaeum, cum tribus latinis interpretationibus et glossis. Genoa, 1516.

Khunrath, Heinrich, Amphitheatrum sapientiae aeternae solius verae, christiano-kabalisticum, divino-magicum, necnon physico-chymicum, tertrinum, catholicon. Hanau, 1609.

Kircher, Athanasius, S.J., Oedipus Aegyptiacus. Rome, 1653.

Knittel, Caspar, S.J., Via regia ad omnes scientias et artes; h.e., Ars universalis scientiarum omnium artiumque arcana facilius penetrandi. Prague, 1682.

Knorr von Rosenroth, Christian, Kabbala denudata seu doctrina Hebraeorum transcendentalis et metaphysica atque theologica. Sulzbach, 1677.

Lagneus, David, Harmonia chemica (1611), in Zetzner, Lazarus, ed., Theatrum chemicum, IV (Strassburg, 1613), 798–910.

Langius, Johannes Michael, De charactere primaevo bibliorum Ebraicorum. Altdorf, 1685.*

Lauret, Christophorus, Hazoar; sive, Illustratio prophetarum de plenitudine temporis Messiae. Paris, 1610.

Lazarelli, Lodovico, Crater hermetis. Paris, 1505.

Lebenwald, Adam, Von des Teufels List und Betrug in der Hebräer Cabbala, Astrologia Judiciaria und Goldmachen. Salzburg, 1680–82.*

Le Loyer, Pierre, Discours, et histoires des spectres, visions et apparitions des esprits, anges, demons et ames se monstrans visibles aux hommes. Paris, 1605.

Lent, Johann von, Schediasma historico-philologicum de Judaeorum Pseudo-Messiis. Herborn, 1683.

Leusden, Johannes, Philologus Hebraeus, continens quaestiones Hebraicas quae circa vetus testamentum Hebraeum fere moveri solent. Utrecht, 1686.

Libavius, Andreas, Tractatus duo physici. Frankfort, 1584.*

Lobkowitz, Johann C., Cabbalae theologicae excidium, prefaced to Aquinas, Thomas, Summa contra gentiles, Hebrew translation by Joseph Ciantes, Rome, 1657.

—— Cabalae totius brevissimum specimen, appended to Puteanus, Erycius, De anagrammatismo, Brussels, 1643.

Longo, Lorenzo (Ranutius Longelus), Caballa anagrammatica. Piacenza, 1654.*

Luther, Martin, Duo D.M. Lutheri fragmenta . . . ad J. Reuchlin De arte cabalistica libros iii. Helmstedt, 1730.

[Mainard, Peter], Opusculum Raymundinum de auditu kabbalistico; sive, Ad omnes scientias introductorium. Venice, 1518.

Marius, Leonard, Commentariorum in universam S. Scripturam. Cologne, 1621.

Menestrier, Cl. François, S.J., La Philosophie des images enigmatiques. Lyons, 1694.

Menochio, Giovanni Stefano, S.J., Le stuore, overo trattenimenti eruditi . . . tessute di varia eruditione, sacra, morale, e profana. Parte prima. Bologna, 1678.

Mersenne, Marin, Observationes et emendationes ad Francisci Georgii Veneti problemata; in hoc opere, cabala evertitur, editio vulgata et inquisitores sanctae fidei catholicae ab haereticorum atque politicorum calumniis accurate vindicantur. Paris, 1623.

—— Quaestiones celeberrimae in Genesim cum accurata textus explicatione. Paris, 1623.

Montecuccolus, Carolus, In cabalam introductio quaedam. Modena, 1612.

More, Henry, A Conjectural Essay of Interpreting the Mind of Moses according to a Threefold Cabbala, viz., Literal, Philosophical, Mystical, or Divinely Moral. London, 1662.

Morestellus, Petrus, Artis kabbalisticae; sive, Sapientia divinae academia. Paris, 1669.*

Naudé, Gabriel, Apologie pour tous les grands personnages qui ont esté faussement soupçonnez de magie. Paris, 1625.

Neander, Michael, Testimonia veterum Hebraeorum, Rabbinorum, Tal-
    mudistarum ac cabbalistarum, de Christo, Mundi Jesua sive Salvatore,
    ad calcem erotematum linguae Hebraeae. Basel, 1567.
Obicius, Hypolitus, Dialogus tripartitus. Venice, 1605.*
Pantheus, Joannes A., Ars transmutationis metallicae. Venice, 1518.
—— Voarchadumia contra alchimiam: ars distincta ab archimia et
    sophia. Venice, 1530.*
Paracelsus, Aurelius Philippus Theophrastus Bombastus, Opera omnia,
    medico-chemico-chirurgica, tribus voluminibus comprehensa. Geneva,
    1662.
—— The Hermetic and Alchemical Writings; English translation by
    A. E. Waite. London, 1894.
—— Sämtliche Werke, ed. by Karl Sudhoff. Munich and Berlin, 1922–
    33. 14 vols.
Paul, Elchanan, Mysterium novum; ein neu herrlich Beweiss aus den
    prophetischen Schriften nach der Hebräer Cabala, dass der Name
    Jesus Christus Gottes Sohn . . . in den fürnehmsten Prophezeiungen
    von Messia verdeckt bedeutet. Helmstedt, 1580.
Pererius, Benedictus, S.J., Adversus fallaces et superstitiosas artes; id est,
    De magia, de observatione somniorum, et de divinatione astrologica,
    libri iii. Venice, 1592.
Peucer, Caspar, Commentarius de praecipuis divinationum generibus, in
    quo a prophetiis, authoritate divina traditis, et a physicis coniecturis,
    discernuntur artes et imposturae diabolicae. Frankfort, 1593.
Pfeiffer, August, Opera omnia quae extant philologica. Utrecht, 1704.
Pico della Mirandola, G., Opera omnia. Basel, 1572.
Pistorius, Johannes, Artis cabalisticae, h.e., Reconditae theologiae et
    philosophiae scriptorum, in quo praeter Pauli Ricii theologicos et
    philosophicos libros sunt Latini pene omnes et Hebraeorum praestantis-
    simi scriptores qui artem commentariis suis illustraverunt. Basel, 1587.
Postel, Guillaume, Abrahami patriarchae liber Jezirah; sive, Formationis
    mundi, patribus quidem Abrahami tempore revelatus, sed ab ipso etiam
    Abrahamo expositus Isaaco, et per profetarum manus posteritati con-
    servatus . . . Vertebat ex Hebraeis et commentariis illustrabat . . .
    Gulielmus Postellus Restitutus. Paris, 1552.
—— De orbis terrae concordia libri iv. Paris, 1544.
—— Histoire et consideration de l'origine, loy, et coutume des Tartares,
    Persiens, Arabes, Turcs, et tous autres Ismaelites ou Muhamediques,
    dit par nous Mahometains, ou Sarrazins. Poitiers, 1560.

Puteanus, Erycius, De anagrammatismo, quae cabalae pars est, diatriba. Brussels, 1642.

[Puteus] Archangelus, of Borgo Nuovo, Apologia fratris Archangeli de Burgonovo . . . pro defensione doctrinae Cabalae contra . . . Petrum Garziam episcopum Ussellensem Mirandulam impugnantem sed minime laedentem, et conclusiones cabalisticae numero LXXI secundum opinionem propriam ejusdem Mirandulae ex ipsis Hebraeorum sapientum fundamentis Christianam religionem maxime declarantes. Basel, 1600.

—— Cabalistarum selectiora obscurioraque dogmata; a Ioanne Pico ex eorum commentationibus pridem excerpta et . . . nunc primum luculentissimis interpretationibus illustrata. Venice, 1569.

—— Specchio di salute: dechiaratione sopra il nome di Giesu secondo gli Ebrei cabalisti. Ferrara, 1557.

Reuchlin, Anton, Tabulae viginti, institutiones in linguam sanctam . . . Accessit his exegesis dictionum in Psalmos sex. Basel, 1554.

Reuchlin, Johann, De verbo mirifico libri iii. Basel, 1494.

—— De arte cabalistica libri iii. Basel, 1561.

Ricchieri, Ludovico (Coelius Rhodiginus), Lectionum antiquarum libri xxx. Geneva, 1620.

Ricci, Paul, In cabalistarum, seu allegorizantium eruditionem isagoge. Augsburg, 1515.

—— Philosophica prophetica ac talmudistica pro Christiana veritate tuenda cum iuniori haebreorum synagoga mirabili ingenii acumine disputatio. Augsburg, 1514.

Ritius, Augustus, De motu octavae sphaerae opus mathematica atque philosophia plenum, in quo et complurima platonicorum et antiquae magiae, quam cabalam Hebraei dicunt, dogmata videre licet. Trino, 1513.*

Rittangel, Iohannes Stefanus, De veritate religionis Christianae . . . pars secunda de Judaeorum cabbala, qua S. Scripturam interpretantur. Franeker, 1699.

—— Liber Jezirah qui Abrahamo patriarchae adscribitur, una cum commentario Rabi Abraham F.D. super 32 semitis sapientiae, a quibus liber Jezirah incipit; translatus et notis illustratus. Amsterdam, 1652.

Rivet, André, Exercitationes CXC in Genesim. Leyden, 1633.

Schickardt, Wilhelm, Bechinat Happeruschim; h.e., Examinis commentationum rabbinicarum in Mosem. Tübingen, 1624.

Schott, Gaspare, S.J., Physica curiosa; sive, Mirabilia naturae et artis libris xii comprehensa. Herbipolis, 1667.

Scot, Reginald, The Discoverie of Witchcraft. London, 1584.

Sennert, Andreas, Exercitationum philologicarum. Wittenberg, 1678.

Smith, Henry, Works, Including Sermons, Treatises, Prayers, and Poems. Edinburgh, 1876.

Spencer, John, De legibus Hebraeorum ritualibus et earum rationibus libri iii. The Hague, 1686.

Sperber, Julius, Kabalisticae precationes. Magdeburg, 1600.

Steeb, Iohann C., Coelum sephiroticum Hebraeorum per portas intelligentiae Moysi revelatas, interiores naturalium rerum characteres . . . ex vetustissima Hebraica veritate . . . explicans. Mainz, 1679.

Steidner, Johann, Jüdische ABC Schul von dem Geheimniss des dreyeinigen wahren Gottes und Schöpfers Jehova. Augsburg, 1665.

Uchtmann, Allard, ed. and tr., Bechinat ha-olam by Jedaiah Penini ben Abraham Bedarsi. Leyden, 1668.

Uythage, Cnaeus C., Revelatio punctationis dissertatio. Leyden, 1680.

Valentinus, Johannes, De triplici Ebraeorum cabbala: gematrija, notarjekon et themura dissertatio. Wittenberg, 1699.

Vallesius, Franciscus, De iis, quae scripta sunt physice in libris sacris; sive, De sacra philosophia liber singularis. Turin, 1587.

Vaughan, Thomas, Anima magica abscondita; or, A Discourse of the universall Spirit of Nature, with his Strange, Abstruse, Miraculous Ascent, and Descent. London, 1650.

—— Anthroposophia theomagica: or, A Discourse of the Nature of Man, and His State after Death; Grounded on His Creator's Protochimistry, and Verifi'd by a Practicall Examination of Principles in the Great World. London, 1656.

Vitringa, Campegius, Sacrarum observationum libri ii. Franeker, 1689.

Voisin, Joseph, Disputatio cabalistica R. Israel filii R. Mosis de Anima adjectis commentariis ex Zohar aliisque rabbinorum libris. Paris, 1635.

—— Observationes in prooemium Pugionis fidei. Prefaced to Martin, Raymond, Pugio fidei. Leipzig, 1687.

SECONDARY SOURCES

Abelson, Joshua, Jewish Mysticism. London, 1913.

Abrahams, Israel, Jewish Life in the Middle Ages. Philadelphia, 1896.

Adler, A., "Die Kabbalah oder die Religionsphilosophie der Hebräer, von A. Franck," *Jahrbücher für spekulative Philosophie*, I (1846), 183–98; 211–21. II (1847), 175–91; 385–93.

Allen, P. S., Opvs epistolarvm Des. Erasmi Roterodami. Oxford, 1908–40.

Anagnine, Eugenio, G. Pico della Mirandola, Sincretismo religioso-filosofico, 1463–1494. Bari, 1937.

Asín y Palacios, Miguel, Abenmasarra y su escuela; orígenes de la filosofía Hispano-Musulmana. Madrid, 1914.

—— "Mohhidin," in Homenaje a Menéndez y Pelayo. Madrid, 1899.

Assemani, Stephen, and Joseph Assemani, Bibliothecae apostolicae Vaticanae codicum manuscriptorum catalogus; partis primae, tomus primus, complectens codices Ebraicos et Samaritanos. Rome, 1756. Facsimile reprint, Paris, 1926.

Baron, Salo Wittmayer, A Social and Religious History of the Jews. New York, 1937.

—— Bibliography of Jewish Social Studies, 1938–39. New York, 1941. Jewish Social Studies Publications, No. 1.

Barth, Friedrich, Die Cabbala des Heinrich Cornelius Agrippa von Nettesheim. Vollständig aus dessen Werke: "De occulta Philosophia." Stuttgart, 1855.

Bauch, G., Geschichte der Leipziger Frühhumanisten. Leipzig, 1899. Beiheft XXII zum *Zentralblatt für Bibliothekswesen*.

Bennett, Charles A., A Philosophical Study of Mysticism: An Essay. New Haven (Conn.), 1923.

Bension, Ariel, The Zohar in Moslem and Christian Spain. London, 1932.

Bevan, Edwyn R., and Charles Singer, The Legacy of Israel. Oxford, 1928.

Bischoff, E., Kritische Geschichte der Thalmud Uebersetzung. Frankfort, 1899.

Blanco Soto, Pedro, Estudios de Bibliografía Luliana. Madrid, 1916.

Blau, Joseph L., "Foreshadowings of Phonetics," *The Spoken Word*, III (1935), 11–13.

—— "The Diffusion of the Christian Interpretation of the Cabala in English Literature," *The Review of Religion*, VI (1941–42), 146–68.

—— "Gershom G. Scholem: Major Trends in Jewish Mysticism," *The Review of Religion*, VIII (1943–44), 67–77.

156   BIBLIOGRAPHY

Blavatsky, Helene Petrovna, Isis Unveiled. New York, 1886.

Bloch, Joshua, Hebrew Printing in Naples. New York, 1942.

Bloch, Philipp, Geschichte der Entwickelung der Kabbala und der jüdischen Religionsphilosophie. Trier, 1894.

Bové, Salvador, El Sistema cientifico Lulliano. Barcelona, 1908.

Cahn, Zvi, The Rise of the Karaite Sect; a New Light on the Halakah and Origin of the Karaites. New York, 1937.

Cambridge History of English Literature, The. Cambridge, 1907–16.

Cassirer, Ernest, "Giovanni Pico della Mirandola; a Study in the History of Renaissance Ideas," *Journal of the History of Ideas*, III (1942), 123–44; 319–46.

Cassuto, Umberto, Gli Ebrei a Firenze nell' età del Rinascimento. Florence, 1918.

Christ, Karl, Die Bibliothek Reuchlin in Pforzheim. Leipzig, 1924. Beiheft LII zum *Zentralblatt für Bibliothekswesen.*

Danzel, Theodor Wilhelm, Magie und Geheimwissenschaft in ihrer Bedeutung für Kultur und Kulturgeschichte. Stuttgart, 1924.

De la Nauze, H., "Ueber das Alter und die Entstehung der Kabala," *Magazin für die Philosophie und ihre Geschichte, aus den Jahrbüchern der Akademien angelegt*, I (1778), 243–74.

Digby, Everard, De duplici methodo libri ii, unicam P. Rami methodum refutantes. London, 1580.

Dorez, L., and L. Thuasne, Pic de la Mirandole en France (1485–1488). Paris, 1897.

Dreydorff, Georg, Das System des Johannes Pico Grafen von Mirandula und Concordia. Marburg, 1858.

Dukas, Jules, Recherches sur l'histoire littéraire du quinzième siècle. Paris, 1876.

Erasmus, Desiderius, Opera omnia. Leyden, 1703.

Franck, Adolph, The Kabbalah; or, The Religious Philosophy of the Hebrews. English translation by I. Sossnitz. New York, 1926.

Freudenthal, J., "Beiträge zur Geschichte der englischen Philosophie," *Archiv für Geschichte der Philosophie*, IV (1891), 452–77.

Fuerst, Julius, Bibliotheca Judaica. Leipzig, 1863.

Garin, Eugenio, Giovanni Pico della Mirandola vita e dottrina. Florence, 1937.

Gautier Vignal, Louis, Pic de la Mirandole. Paris, 1937.

Geiger, Ludwig, Johann Reuchlin, sein Leben und seine Werke. Leipzig, 1871.

—— Johann Reuchlins Briefwechsel. Tübingen, 1871. Bibliothek des litterarischen Vereins in Stuttgart, No. 126.

Ginsburg, Christian D., The Kabbalah: Its Doctrine, Development, and Literature. London, 1920.

Goodenough, Edwin R., By Light, Light. The Mystic Gospel of Hellenistic Judaism. New Haven (Conn.), 1935.

Graetz, Heinrich, History of the Jews from the Earliest Times to the Present Day; English translation by B. Loewy. London, 1892.

Güdeman, M., Geschichte des Erziehungswesens und der Cultur der abendländischen Juden während des Mittelalters und der neueren Zeit. Vienna, 1880–88.

Gunkel, Herman, The Legends of Genesis. Chicago, 1907.

Herford, R. Travers, The Pharisees. New York, 1924.

—— Pirke aboth. New York, 1930.

Histoire littéraire de la France. Paris, 1733–1938.

Hopper, Vincent F., Medieval Number Symbolism; Its Sources, Meaning, and Influence on Thought and Expression. New York, 1938.

Jacobs, Joseph, Jewish Contributions to Civilization; an Estimate. Philadelphia, 1920.

James, William, Varieties of the Religious Experience; a Study in Human Nature. New York, 1913.

Jellinek, Adolph, Beiträge zur Geschichte der Kabbala. Leipzig, 1852.

Kahana (Kohan), David, A History of the Cabalists, Shabbetians and Chassidim. Odessa, 1913. In Hebrew.

Karppe, S., Etude sur les origines et la nature de Zohar, précédée d'une étude sur l'histoire de la kabale. Paris, 1901.

Kibre, Pearl, The Library of Pico della Mirandola. New York, 1936.

Kiesewetter, Karl, Der Occultismus des Altertums. Leipzig [1896].

Knight, Samuel, The Life of Dr. John Colet . . . and Several Original Papers relating to the Said Life. London, 1724.

Kristeller, Paul Oskar, "Marsilio Ficino e Lodovico Lazzarelli," *Annali della R. Scuola Normale Superiore di Pisa, Series II*, VII (1938), 237–62.

—— "Anagnine's G. Pico della Mirandola," *Civiltà moderna*, X (1938), 1–4.

Levi, Eliphas, Histoire de la magie. Paris, 1860.

—— La Clef des grands mystères. Paris, 1861.

—— Transcendental Magic; Its Doctrine and Ritual. English translation by A. E. Waite. New York [1938].

Lindstrom, Martin, Philipp Nicolais Kristendomstolkning. Stockholm, 1937.

Marcu, Valeriu, The Expulsion of the Jews from Spain. New York, 1935.

Massetani, G., La filosofia cabbalistica di Giovanni Pico della Mirandola. Empoli, 1897.

Memorie e documenti per la storia dell'Università di Pavia. Pavia, 1878.

Moore, George Foot, Judaism in the First Centuries of the Christian Era, the Age of the Tannaim. Cambridge (Mass.), 1927.

Morley, Henry, The Life of Henry Cornelius Agrippa von Nettesheim, Doctor and Knight, Commonly Known as a Magician. London, 1856.

Müller, Ernst, Der Sohar und seine Lehre; Einleitung in die Gedanken-welt der Kabbala. Vienna, 1923.

Nicolson, Marjorie Hope, "Milton and the *Conjectura cabbalistica*," *The Philological Quarterly*, VI (1927), 1–18.

d'Orliac, Jehan, Francis I, Prince of the Renaissance. Philadelphia, 1932.

Ottaviano, Carmel, L'Ars compendiosa de R. Lulle avec une étude sur la Bibliographie et le Fond Ambrosien de Lulle. Paris, 1930. Etudes de Philosophie Médiévale, No. 12.

Paris, Paulin, Les Manuscrits françois de la Bibliothèque du Roi. Paris, 1848.

Pick, Bernhard, The Cabala; Its Influence on Judaism and Christianity. Chicago, 1913.

Popper, William, The Censorship of Hebrew Books. New York, 1899.

Probst, Jean Henri, Caractère et origine des Idées du Bienheureux Raymond Lulle (Ramon Lull). Toulouse, 1912.

Remusat, C. F. M., Histoire de la philosophie en Angleterre. Paris, 1875.

Schechter, Solomon, Studies in Judaism. Second series. Philadelphia, 1908.

Schnederman, Georg, Die Controverse des Ludovicus Cappellus mit den Buxtorfen über das Alter der hebräischen Punctation. Leipzig, 1878.

Scholem, Gerhard Gershom, Bibliographia Cabbalistica. Leipzig, 1927.

—— Chapters in the Literary History of the Cabala. Jerusalem, 1931. In Hebrew.

—— "Inquiry into the Kabbala of R. Isaac ben Jacob Ha-Cohen," *Tarbiz*, II (1930–31), 188–217, 415–42; III (1931–32), 33–66, 258–86; IV (1932–33), 54–77, 207–25; V (1933–34), 50–60, 180–98, 305–23. In Hebrew.

—— "Kabbala," in Encyclopaedia Judaica, IX, columns 630–732. Berlin, 1932.

—— Major Trends in Jewish Mysticism. Jerusalem, 1941.

—— "Philosophy and Jewish Mysticism," *The Review of Religion*, II (1937–38), 385–402.

—— "Zur Frage der Entstehung der Kabbala," in *Korrespondenzblatt des Vereins zur Gründung und Erhaltung einer Akademie für die Wissenschaft des Judentums*, IX (1928), 4–26.

Scott, Cyril, An Outline of Modern Occultism. New York, 1935.

Seebohm, Frederic, The Oxford Reformers. London [1914].

Semprini, Giovanni, La filosofia di Pico della Mirandola. Milan, 1936.

Senebier, Jean, Catalogue raisonné des manuscrits . . . de Genève. Geneva, 1779.

Silver, Abba Hillel, A History of Messianic Speculation in Israel from the First through the Seventeenth Centuries. New York, 1927.

Sjöberg, Erik, Gott und die Sünder im palästinischen Judentum nach dem Zeugnis der Tannaiten und der apokryphisch-pseudepigraphischen Literatur. Stuttgart, 1939. Beiträge zur Wissenschaft vom alten und neuen Testament, Series IV, No. 27.

Stöckl, Albert, Geschichte der Philosophie des Mittelalters. Mainz, 1865.

Thenaud, Jean, Le Voyage d'outremer (Égypte, Mont Sinay, Palestine) . . . suivi de la relation de l'ambassade de Domenico Trevisan auprès du Soudan d'Égypte, 1512; ed. by C. Schefer. Paris, 1884.

Thorndike, Lynn, A History of Magic and Experimental Science. New York.
   Vol. IV: The Fifteenth Century. 1940.
   Vols. V–VI: The Sixteenth Century. 1941.

Trachtenberg, Joshua, Jewish Magic and Superstition; a Study in Folk Religion. New York, 1939.

Vossler, Karl, Mediaeval Culture; an Introduction to Dante and His Times. New York, 1929.

Vulliaud, Paul, La Kabbale Juive. Paris, 1923.

Wadding, Lucas, Annales minorum. Rome, 1721–94.

Waite, Arthur E., The Holy Kabbalah; a Study of the Secret Tradition in Israel. New York, 1929.

Westcott, William Wynn, An Introduction to the Study of the Kabalah. London, 1926.

INDEX